Peggie Benton

Finnish Food

for

your table

With Illustrations by the Author

BRUNO CASSIRER
OXFORD

© PEGGIE BENTON

1960

TX
723.5
.F5
B45

WIDENER UNIVERSITY
WOLFGRAM
LIBRARY
CHESTER, PA.

Printed in England for
Bruno Cassirer (Publishers) Ltd., Oxford
By Lawrence Bros. (W-s-M) Ltd., London and Weston-super-Mare
Distributed by
Faber & Faber Ltd., 24 Russell Square, London, W.C.1

My warmest thanks are due to Miss Ilta Arvola, and to Mrs. Katri Laine for permission to use recipes from her book, " Ruokatalous "; also to Dorothy M. White for her encouragement, and help in proof reading.

To my severest Critics:

My Family

Contents

Contents

Introduction

FOR several years our home was enlivened by Finnish students who came to this country to learn English and help in the house. While chatting and cooking with these delightful girls I decided to collect the recipes enjoyed by our family and make them into a book.

Soon I became interested in Finland and the extraordinary contrasts it presents. I was told of the Laplanders and their reindeer, and of tall glass and concrete hotels rising out of the forest; of the midnight sun and the great freeze which grips the country during the long winter. Later, I went to Finland and was charmed by what I saw.

Perhaps it is the clarity of the light and the freshness of the air which have sharpened the minds of the Finnish people; just as the solid structure of tradition, like the granite underlying the forests, has formed their character. Finnish architects and interior decorators are pioneers in design, while Finnish craftsmanship is rooted in tradition.

The steady rhythm of the seasons favours creative activity. In spring there is sudden release and a rush and dazzle of growth. Trees and flowers burst into bud, and leaf and bloom. Fruit and grain swell and ripen in the span of a few weeks. There is an urgency of creation, of living and enjoying, scarcely interrupted by the brief twilight nights. All this is followed by the long silence of winter; a time when nature draws back into itself for renewal and people take refuge in the quiet of their homes. Beneath the snow, seeds fallen in the brilliant autumn lie dark and undisturbed.

Like so many women, much of my life is now confined between the walls of a small kitchen and I often think with nostalgia of the vast lakes and forests of Finland and the sparkle of light and water. Every year there are a thousand meals to cook and only a limited choice of food. So, by the evocative use of old materials in different ways I try to escape monotony and re-create the joys of travel.

Note

The recipes which follow have been adapted for English homes. In most cases they serve from four to six people, though it is always difficult to make definite indications where varying appetites are concerned.

If economy is important, margarine can be substituted for butter (but please make it the best margarine) and if time must be saved those with pressure cookers and electric blenders will be able to cut many corners.

The notes on ' Leftovers ' are merely suggestions from a wealth of possibilities. Let us hope you enjoy the food so much that there will be few opportunities.

Soups

The charm of Finnish soups lies in their unusual accompaniments. Delightful partnerships occur, such as carrot soup with prawn dumplings, vegetable soup and cheese sandwiches, or pork soup with prunes. It is amusing to experiment with others.

Pork Soup

This soup is greatly esteemed by the foresters. They make it in large iron cauldrons hung on chains over a wood fire.

1 *lb. fillet of pork*	½ *teaspoon salt*	½ *teaspoon made mustard*
2½ *pints water*	5 *peppercorns*	1 *teaspoon sugar*

Cut the pork in small pieces, season with pepper and salt, and allow it to simmer three or four hours, then lift it out and strain the liquid. Season with sugar and mustard, and add the pork. If the soup is very fat, let it cool before seasoning, skim off the fat and re-heat. Serve with boiled prunes and pieces of pastry.

LEFTOVERS: Use the liquid as stock, and the meat fried with vegetables.

Liver Soup

¼ *lb. calf's liver*	2 *ozs. butter*	1 *oz. white bread*
3 *pints stock*	2 *ozs. flour*	1 *yolk of egg* *salt*

Cut the liver in neat pieces, roll these in flour and fry them in butter together with the bread, cut in squares. When the pieces of liver are nicely browned, mince them and put them into the stock to boil. Put them through a sieve, re-heat, and just before serving, pour the soup onto the beaten yolk of egg. Garnish with fried bread.

LEFTOVERS: Mix with minced ham, breadcrumbs and seasoning, and pile on hot buttered toast.

Week-Day Soup

1 *lb. cold meat*	1 *lb. potatoes*	1 *bay leaf*
2½ *pints water*	1 *small onion*	*salt*

Peel the potatoes, cut them in pieces and put them in a pan with the meat. Add the water with sliced onions and bay leaf, and bring to the boil. Cook until the potatoes are done, and add the salt. Serve with pieces of bread and butter spread with cheese.

LEFTOVERS: Mix with milk and eggs and use for meat puddings.

Blood Soup

This is considered a great delicacy in Finland.

1 *small fat chicken*	*a piece of root ginger*	2 *apples*
4 *ozs. fresh pork*	1 *small onion*	
4 *pints water*	½ *pint calf's or pig's blood*	
10 *cooked prunes*	½ *tablespoon flour*	
¼ *teaspoon powdered cloves*	*sugar, salt and vinegar*	

Clean the chicken, cut it in pieces and put it in a saucepan with pork, ginger and onion. Cover with water, bring to the boil, and simmer for four hours. Lift out the chicken and pork, and put the liquid through a sieve. Mix the flour and blood, pour it into the boiling soup and beat until it boils again. Then add the chicken, pork and prunes, the apples peeled and cut in pieces, and the cloves, sugar and vinegar. Allow the soup to boil gently for a short time. If the soup should boil too long the blood will curdle. Serve very hot with pieces of fried bread.

LEFTOVERS: Use the meat for rissoles or stuffing and the liquid for stock.

Economical Fish Soup

This soup is very economical, as it may be made from the head, tail, bones and scraps of any raw fish. Salmon is particularly delicious.

5 *pints water*
pieces of any fresh raw fish
a piece of celery
1 *carrot*
1 *onion*

1 *lb. fresh or a small packet of*
  frozen peas
pepper and salt
1 *tablespoon chopped parsley*
4 *ozs. cream*

Put the fish and the chopped prepared vegetables, except the peas, into the water and bring to the boil. Simmer for two hours. Lift out the fish bones, and put the soup through a sieve. Bring to the boil and add the peas. When the peas are cooked season carefully. Beat the cream and add it just before serving. Sprinkle with chopped parsley. Serve with cheese biscuits.

LEFTOVERS: Use the liquid for fish sauce and the vegetables for fish puddings.

Herring Soup

3 *split and boned fresh herrings*
2½ *pints water*   1 *tablespoon flour*   1 *small carrot*
1 *teaspoon salt*   1 *tablespoon butter*   1 *stick of celery*
5 *peppercorns*   1 *onion*   2 *potatoes*
½ *tablespoon chopped parsley*   *a pinch of grated nutmeg*

Cut the vegetables in pieces and bring to the boil with the seasoning. When they are nearly done, add the flour made into a paste with the cold water, and the herrings cut into small pieces. When the herrings are cooked pour the soup into a bowl, add the butter and sprinkle with parsley. Serve with slices of toast.

LEFTOVERS: Drain the fish and vegetables and use for rissoles.

Cabbage Soup

In the farm houses a soup of this kind, followed by a bowl of porridge, often forms the whole mid-day meal.

half a cabbage   3 *pints water*   2 *ozs. butter*
1 *lb. scrag of mutton or*   1 *tablespoon flour*   *salt and pepper*
  lamb

Wash the meat, cut it in pieces, and put it with the bone into cold water. Bring the soup to the boil. Let it simmer for two hours. Cut the cabbage in pieces and fry it until nicely brown. Add the stock and allow it to simmer for about an hour. Remove the bones and serve the soup in a deep dish, leaving the pieces of meat whole. This soup may also be made using bones only, and served with forcemeat balls instead of meat.

LEFTOVERS: Use the liquid as stock, and the meat and cabbage to fill pasties.

Carrot Soup

1½ *lbs. carrots*   1 *pint milk*   ½ *tablespoon flour*
½ *pint water*   1 *oz. butter*   *salt, sugar and nutmeg*
½ *tablespoon chopped parsley*

Wash the carrots, cut them in pieces, and throw them into slightly salted water. Bring to the boil and simmer about half an hour. Melt the butter and mix in the flour. Cook these together for a few minutes, then add the warmed milk gradually. Put the carrots through a sieve, mix them with the water in which they have been boiled, and the white sauce. Put the soup into a hot tureen, sprinkle with chopped parsley, and serve with prawn or vegetable balls (pages 9–10).

LEFTOVERS: Thicken with mashed potato and use as a vegetable.

Pea Soup

2 *pints dried peas*   ½ *lb. pork*   *a piece of ginger*
4 *pints stock or water*   *salt*

Put the peas, two pints of stock or water and the salt into a saucepan and bring them to the boil. When the water has nearly evaporated, add the last two pints of water and the pork, cut in squares. When the peas are cooked, skim off the skins which have risen to the top, and season the soup. Serve with mustard and pieces of fried bread.

LEFTOVERS: Put through a sieve and make a cream soup adding water and milk, or a little cream.

Rice Soup

2½ *pints meat or vegetable stock*   3 *ozs. rice*
1 *tablespoon grated cheese*

Put the rice into boiling salted water. Remove it from the fire, then bring it to the boil again. Repeat this twice. Drain, and pour cold water over the rice. Bring the stock to the boil, add the rice and simmer for an hour. Pour it into a hot tureen and sprinkle with grated cheese. Serve with cheese sticks (page 7).

LEFTOVERS: Use the rice for savoury fillings or fish cakes and the liquid as a soup, refreshed by the addition of vegetables.

Summer Vegetable Soup

1 *lb. vegetables (small carrots, peas, pieces of cauliflower, etc.)*
1 *pint water*   1½ *tablespoons flour*   *salt, sugar, nutmeg*
2 *pints milk*   2 *ozs. butter*   ½ *tablespoon chopped parsley*
2 *ozs. cooked prawns (optional)*

Clean the vegetables and cut them in pieces. Put them in lightly salted water and bring them to the boil. Simmer about half an hour. Melt the butter, stir in the flour, cook them well together, and mix in gradually the warmed milk. Add the vegetables with their stock, and, if possible, some prawns. Pour the soup into a hot tureen, and sprinkle with chopped parsley. Serve with cheese sandwiches.

LEFTOVERS: Use the vegetables, sieved, for a mould. Season the liquid and use as stock.

Vegetable Soup

2½ *pints clear*   1 *tablespoon butter*   1 *egg*
   vegetable stock   2 *tablespoons flour*   2 *ozs. cream*

Melt the butter in a saucepan, and stir in the flour over a gentle fire. Mix the stock in gradually, and allow it to boil ten minutes. Beat the egg and cream in a bowl and add the soup, beating all the time. Serve with fish balls (page 9) or cheese dumplings (page 8).

LEFTOVERS: Use as a sauce with a handful of fresh, chopped parsley.

Mashed Potato Soup

3 *pints meat or vegetable stock, or water*   2 *lbs. small potatoes*
2 *tablespoons rice*   1 *tablespoon sago*   2 *yolks of egg*
2 *tablespoons vermicelli*   4 *ozs. cream or evaporated milk*
1 *tablespoon chopped parsley*

Cook the potatoes in stock. Lift out half of them, and mash the rest. Add the sago, rice and vermicelli, and allow the soup to simmer until they are cooked. Beat the yolks of eggs and cream in a basin, and pour the soup over them. Add lastly, the whole potatoes and chopped parsley. This soup is sometimes eaten instead of boiled potatoes as an accompaniment to meat. Cold cooked potatoes can be mashed and used for this soup, one pound of small potatoes being freshly cooked and left whole.

LEFTOVERS: Add more potatoes well mashed with a lump of butter and some freshly ground black pepper and use as a vegetable.

Accompaniments to Soup

A large bowl of soup with dumplings or fish balls makes a hot, sustaining meal for a winter day, or a good supper dish. When omelets or dumplings are eaten with soup, it need seldom be followed by a meat course.

Cheese and Chives

8 *ozs. grated cheese*   1 *tablespoon chopped chives*

Mix the cheese and the chives and sprinkle them over meat or vegetable soup. They may also be served separately.

LEFTOVERS: Use for filling omelets or flavouring sauces.

Fried Bread

6 *slices of white bread*   ½ *pint milk*   1 *oz. butter*

Remove the crusts from the slices of bread, dip them in milk and fry them in butter. Serve hot with meat and vegetable soups.

LEFTOVERS: On cooling the slices become rather tough and are of little further interest.

Cheese Toast

6 *slices of white toast*   2 *ozs. grated cheese*   1 *white of egg*

Beat the white of egg and mix it with the grated cheese. Spread a layer of the mixture on each piece of toast, and put them under the grill until the whites are set, and the tops golden brown. Serve with meat, fish, and vegetable soup.

LEFTOVERS: Cut into small triangles and top with strips of anchovy and capers or chopped hard-boiled egg. Use as canapés with cocktails.

Baked Omelet

4 eggs   2 ozs. butter
4 ozs. cream or evaporated milk   salt and pepper

Beat the eggs and add the beaten cream and seasoning. Put the mixture into a greased fireproof dish, and bake in the oven. Serve with meat, vegetable, and milk soups.

LEFTOVERS: Use sliced in a cold vegetable salad.

Soup Pancakes

6 ozs. milk   1 egg   salt
2 ozs. flour   ½ tablespoon grated cheese   1 oz. butter

Beat the egg and add milk, flour and salt. Beat the mixture well, and let it stand two hours. Fry thin pancakes in butter, sprinkle them with cheese, turn and fry on the other side. Serve hot with meat and vegetable soups.

LEFTOVERS: Fill with creamed spinach, mushroom or chicken etc., roll and brown in the oven, covered with grated cheese and dabs of butter or a piquant sauce.

Potato Sticks

½ pint mashed potatoes   1 large egg or two small
2 ozs. flour   salt, nutmeg and breadcrumbs

Mix the flour and the yolk and part of the white of the egg gradually into the mashed potatoes. Season the mixture, and make it into sticks about the length and thickness of a finger. Coat them with beaten white of egg, and sprinkle with breadcrumbs. Cook on a baking sheet, and serve hot with meat or vegetable soup.

LEFTOVERS: Re-heat and eat with butter and cheese.

Cheese Sticks

2 ozs. milk   ½ lb. flour   salt
1 oz. butter   2 ozs. grated cheese   ¼ teaspoon soda
1 large or two small eggs

Beat one egg, add milk, melted butter, half the grated cheese and the salt, flour and soda. Mix well, and form into sticks as above. Coat with egg and grated cheese and brown in the oven. Serve with meat and vegetable soups.

LEFTOVERS: Re-heat, spread with any savoury paste, and use as canapés.

Sand Sticks

4 ozs. milk	1 oz. cornflour	salt
3 eggs	4 ozs. flour	½ teaspoon soda
grated rind of one lemon		

Beat the eggs and set a little aside for coating. Add the milk, seasoning, cornflour and ordinary flour. Mix well and make into sticks. Coat them with beaten egg and bake. Serve with meat, fish and vegetable soups.

LEFTOVERS: Crumble and use instead of breadcrumbs.

Barley or Oatmeal Dumplings

| 4 ozs. butter | 8 ozs. rolled oats or barley |
| 3 eggs | salt |

Beat the butter until creamy and stir in gradually the eggs, oats or barley, and salt. Drop spoonfuls into boiling meat or vegetable soup, and allow them to simmer fifteen minutes. Serve hot with meat or vegetable soup.

LEFTOVERS: Mix into meat puddings or rissoles.

Bread Dumplings

3 ozs. white breadcrumbs	3 yolks of egg
3 tablespoons melted butter	sugar and nutmeg
3 tablespoons cream or milk	

Mix the breadcrumbs with the butter and beat until white and creamy. Add the cream, yolks of egg and seasoning, and mix well. Drop small spoonfuls into boiling meat or vegetable soup.

LEFTOVERS: Re-heat and serve with tomato sauce and rolls of grilled bacon.

Cheese Dumplings

| 1 pint milk   salt | 2 ozs. flour | 3 yolks of egg |
| 2 ozs. butter | 3 eggs, well beaten | 2 ozs. grated cheese |

Bring the milk to the boil and add the butter and flour. Allow the mixture to boil ten minutes, beating all the time. Remove it to cool, and add the beaten eggs, the yolks of egg and the cheese. Season the mixture and drop with a spoon into boiling soup. Simmer a few minutes and serve hot with the soup.

LEFTOVERS: Chop the dumplings and warm them in a savoury tomato sauce.

Flour Dumplings

3 *eggs*   *salt*
their weight in flour and butter

Beat the butter till creamy; then add gradually the eggs, flour and salt. Cook in small balls in boiling meat or vegetable soup. When done lift them out, keep them hot and serve with the soup.

LEFTOVERS: Use in making meat puddings.

Potato Dumplings

4 *ozs. cooked potatoes*   2 *ozs. butter*   2 *ozs. flour*
4 *ozs. breadcrumbs*   1 *egg*   *salt, sugar and nutmeg*

Mash the potatoes. Add the butter, breadcrumbs, flour and seasoning. Mix well, form into small balls with a spoon and drop into boiling meat or vegetable soup.

LEFTOVERS: Use for potato cakes.

Fish or Prawn Balls

12 *ozs. cooked fish or prawns*   2 *ozs. butter*   3 *eggs*
4 *ozs. breadcrumbs*   *salt, sugar and nutmeg*

Mix the pounded fish or prawns well into the butter. Add the yolks of egg, breadcrumbs, seasoning and lastly, the whites beaten to a stiff froth. Cook small balls of the mixture in boiling fish or prawn soup. After a few minutes, drain and serve hot.

LEFTOVERS: Use for filling omelets or mix with anchovy sauce and serve browned, in scallop shells.

Raisin Dumplings

1 *egg*   8 *ozs. cream or milk*   2 *ozs. raisins*
1½ *tablespoons sugar*   6 *ozs. breadcrumbs*   *salt*

Beat the egg; add the sugar, cream, breadcrumbs and raisins and season with salt. If the dumplings break, bind them with a little flour. They may be cooked in meat soups, or in boiling salted water. They make an excellent accompaniment to meat soup.

LEFTOVERS: Re-heat and use with roast meat.

Vegetable Balls

12 *ozs. cooked sieved vegetables*   *onion*   3 *eggs*
2 *ozs. butter*   4 *ozs. breadcrumbs*   *salt and sugar*

Mash the drained vegetables well; add the onion fried golden brown in butter, the yolks of egg, breadcrumbs and seasoning. Let the mixture stand, and then fold in the beaten whites of egg. Drop small spoonfuls of the mixture into boiling meat or vegetable soup and cook for a few minutes.

LEFTOVERS: Chop the balls, add a little cream, and use for filling omelets.

Fish

Of all the varieties of fish used in this country, only a few can be obtained in Finland. Of these, the chief are salmon, herring, hake and flounder.

Salmon is very plentiful in the rivers of North Finland. The fishermen net them in great quantities, usually lifting and laying the nets at sunset. In country places, the salmon are sold whole and then are either salted or divided up, the best cuts being fried or stuffed, the rougher pieces used for puddings, and the bones and scraps for soup or fish jelly. Fresh salmon skin is delicious grilled, and eaten with red pepper and lemon juice. This is considered a great delicacy in Finland.

The skin of salmon or any large fish is often dried in the sun until it is quite silvery and without smell. It is kept in jars, and a little piece broken off, and put in the kettle when coffee is brewed. This makes the coffee as clear and sparkling as wine.

Herring are imported into Finland, and are always salted or smoked, but the place of fresh herring is taken by a small fish called Silakka or Baltic herring. The recipes for fresh herring which follow should really be made with Silakka, but as the flavours are similar, ordinary herring may be used instead.

10

Quantities of fresh fish are caught in the lakes. Great lines, a kilometre long, with hooks hanging from them at intervals of several feet, are laid on buoys at night. At sunrise, the lines are lifted from a boat, and the catch is usually fried in butter or salted in wooden tubs.

There are many tree-covered islands in the Finnish lakes. At holiday time people row out to the islands and build great fires of pine branches. Over the fire they sling on crossed boughs the coffee kettle and a large iron pot. Fresh-caught fish are cleaned and cut up, and thrown into the pot with water and salt. After hard rowing or a plunge in the clear water, everyone sits round the fire and eats stewed fish, to the smell of wood smoke and coffee, pungent in the brilliant fresh air.

Fillets of Flounder

Flounder is not very much used in England as it is rather coarse, but it is the only flat fish obtainable in Finland. Plaice or sole may be used for this recipe.

1½ lbs. fillets of flounder, plaice or sole
4 ozs. flour	4 ozs. butter	2 eggs salt
breadcrumbs	10 bitter almonds	1 onion

Mix the flour, chopped almonds and salt, and coat the fillets. Brush them over with beaten egg and breadcrumbs. Slice the onions, and brown them in butter. Remove the onions from the pan, and fry the fillets in the remaining fat. Serve with fried onion or currant sauce (pages 73 and 72), potatoes and prunes.

LEFTOVERS: Serve the fillets cold with slices of lemon.

Hake with Ale

1½ lbs. hake	1 bay leaf	a bunch of parsley
½ sliced lemon	a piece of ginger	1 pint of ale
1 onion	carrot	½ pint of water
5 peppercorns	half a stick of celery	½ tablespoon salt

Put the water and ale into a saucepan and add the seasoning, onions, sliced lemon and the vegetables cut in pieces. Allow them to simmer for an hour, and then cool a little. Put the fish in the pan and cook it gently until the fins come away easily. Serve immediately with potatoes, fried tomatoes or spinach balls, sour-sweet sauce (page 71) or mayonnaise.

LEFTOVERS: Serve cold with mayonnaise.

Hake with Horse-radish Sauce

1½ lbs. hake or a whole white fish of that weight
½ lemon   ½ tablespoon salt   horse-radish sauce
onion   water   grated horse-radish

Put the water, salt and sliced lemon in a saucepan and boil for ten minutes. Remove the pan from the fire and when cool, put in the fish and poach it for about a quarter of an hour or until the fins are easily detachable. The fish must be served directly it is cooked. It is better to leave the scales on the fish as this improves the flavour. Serve with potatoes, spinach and horse-radish sauce. The sauce should be mixed with cream so that its flavour is rather mild, and a separate dish of grated horse-radish put on the table.

LEFTOVERS: Remove the bones from the cold fish and use it for fish cakes or salad.

Stuffed Hake

a hake weighing about 2 lbs.   2 fillets of anchovy
the white of one egg   salt   onion
breadcrumbs   4 ozs. prunes   1 egg
4 ozs. butter   4 ozs. rice   water

Cook the rice and prunes separately. Brown the onion in butter and mix it with the cooked rice and prunes, the anchovies cut in pieces, and the egg. Scrape the scales from the fish, slit it open, fill it with the mixture, and sew it up. Lay the hake in a greased fireproof dish, coat it with white of egg, and sprinkle it with salt and breadcrumbs. Bake in an oven pre-heated to 350° and when it is nicely browned, add a little boiling water and baste occasionally. Use the liquor in the dish as sauce and serve the fish with potatoes, salad or spinach.

LEFTOVERS: Remove the bones from the fish and cover it with mayonnaise.

Fried Hake

one hake weighing about 2 lbs.   1 calf's kidney or 2 sheep's kidneys
1 egg   salt   4 ozs. prunes   water and vinegar
breadcrumbs   1 small teaspoon sugar   lard or dripping

Cook the kidneys in water to which a tablespoonful of vinegar has been added, and when cooked chop them finely. Boil the prunes, remove the stones, chop, and add them with the salt and sugar to the kidneys. Scrape the hake, open and fill it with the stuffing. Sew it up, and curl it round with its tail in its mouth. Coat with salted egg and breadcrumbs. Make the fat smoking hot and fry the fish in it, turning it once when the underneath is cooked. Garnish with hard-boiled eggs, and serve with sour-sweet sauce (page 71), potatoes and vegetables.

LEFTOVERS: After removing the bones, use for fish cakes.

Cold Garnished Hake

a hake to weigh about 2 lbs.	salt and bay leaf
2 tablespoons vinegar	

FOR GARNISHING

¼ pint cream	½ lemon	1 tablespoon grated horse-radish
½ cooked beetroot		5 small cooked mushrooms
parsley		cochineal

Put the water, vinegar, bay leaf and salt in a saucepan. When nearly boiling put in the fish, poach about a quarter of an hour and when done, remove the skin. Lay the hake on a dish to cool, and prepare the garnish. Whip the cream, mix in the grated horse-radish, and colour with fresh beetroot juice or cochineal. Pour the cream over the fish and decorate with small mushrooms, chopped beetroot, slices of lemon, and parsley. Serve at once with boiled potatoes.

LEFTOVERS: Remove the bones from the fish, cut it in small pieces, mix with mayonnaise and serve as fish salad with lettuce, cucumber or tomato.

Grilled Herring

Grill split herrings and when done, pour over them melted butter, and sprinkle with chopped chives. Serve with egg sauce and potatoes or vegetables.

Fried Herring Fillets

3 large split herrings	breadcrumbs	2 large onions
2 eggs	4 ozs. butter	

Coat the herrings with beaten egg and breadcrumbs and fry them in butter. Slice the onions, brown them in butter, and pile some on each fillet. Serve with currant sauce (page 72), potatoes and spinach.

LEFTOVERS: Pour a little vinegar over the herrings and after they have stood two days, serve them with chopped hard-boiled egg.

13

Herring Salad

The potatoes should be cooked in their skins and all the vegetables diced when they are cold.

1 *cooked herring*	1 *diced gherkin*
½ *lb. cooked beetroot*	1 *diced apple*
6 *ozs. cooked carrot*	1 *hard-boiled egg*
6 *ozs. cooked potatoes*	1 *gill sour cream (or cream and*
6 *ozs. cold cooked meat*	*yoghurt) salt and pepper*

Clean the herring, remove the skin and bones, and cut it in small pieces. Set a little of the carrot and beetroot aside for garnishing. Mix the rest together with the diced potatoes and season with salt and pepper. Arrange in a mound on a dish, moisten with some sour cream, or yoghurt mixed with cream, and decorate with chopped egg, beetroot and carrot.

Herring Stew

2 *split and boned herrings*	4 *ozs. breadcrumbs*	4 *ozs. butter*
½ *pint cream or evaporated*	*pepper and sugar*	2 *eggs*
milk		

Put the herrings through a sieve, or cream in an electric blender, and fry the purée in butter. Add the breadcrumbs and cream gradually and allow the mixture to boil for ten minutes. Season it with pepper and a trace of sugar. Add, lastly, the chopped hard-boiled eggs, and serve with potatoes.

LEFTOVERS: Pile on hot buttered toast and brown under the grill.

Herring Cooked in Paper

3 *filleted herrings*

Wrap every fillet in greaseproof paper or foil and cook in a good oven for about 10 minutes. Serve the herrings wrapped, and eat them hot with potatoes and currant sauce.

LEFTOVERS: Chop the herrings and use for salad, with cold sliced potatoes, finely chopped onion and sliced apple.

Red Herrings with Egg

2 *red herrings*	1 *hard-boiled egg*	*melted butter*

Soak the herrings overnight in cold water. Skin and then split them and remove the bones. Put the slices in a dish, pour boiling water over them, and let them stand a moment. Then drain off the water and repeat the process two or three times.

Pour melted butter over the herring, sprinkle with chopped hard-boiled egg and serve with potatoes.

Red Herring with Mayonnaise

3 red herrings   *4 eggs*   *mayonnaise sauce*

Prepare the herrings as before. Arrange them in a dish and cover with mayonnaise. Garnish with slices of hard-boiled egg and serve with potatoes or vegetables.

Lobster Pudding

¼ lb. lobster meat fresh, frozen or tinned   *4 ozs. butter*   *3 eggs*
½ pint cream or evaporated milk   *4 ozs. breadcrumbs*
salt and pepper

Put the lobster through a mincer and add the cream, whipped, the breadcrumbs, seasoning and beaten yolks of egg. Beat until the mixture is creamy and then fold in the whites of egg beaten to a stiff froth. Steam the mixture for one hour in a greased basin which has been sprinkled with breadcrumbs, and serve with hollandaise sauce and toast.

In Finland this pudding is made with crayfish which are found in the rivers.

LEFTOVERS: Cut in slices and serve cold.

Stuffed Salmon

Where salmon is plentiful, this dish is usually made with a whole fish, but a large cut may quite well be used instead.

about 2 lbs. salmon   *4 ozs. prunes*
4 ozs. butter   *2 ozs. rice or 4 ozs. mushrooms*

Stuff the fish with chopped, cooked prunes mixed with boiled rice, or fried mushrooms which have been seasoned with salt and a trace of sugar. Tie it round carefully and lay it in a greased fireproof dish. Brush over with beaten egg and sprinkle with salt. Cover with greased paper and cook in an over pre-heated to 325° for from 35 to 45 minutes. During the baking baste occasionally. Serve with potatoes, prunes or cooked peas, and mayonnaise sauce.

LEFTOVERS: Remove the bones from the salmon, mix it with rice and beaten egg, shape it into balls and fry; or eat cold with salad.

15

Fried Salmon Steaks

2 lbs. salmon steaks	4 ozs. flour	sugar and salt
2 eggs	breadcrumbs	4 ozs. butter

Brush the steaks with lemon juice, and sprinkle them with salt and a trace of sugar. Coat them in flour, egg and breadcrumb, and fry golden brown in butter. Serve with mayonnaise, potatoes, prunes and cooked peas.

LEFTOVERS: Dress the cold salmon with mayonnaise and eat it with salad.

Grilled Salmon Steaks

1½ lbs. salmon steaks	4 ozs. butter	1 onion
1 tablespoon chopped parsley		salt and sugar

Brown the finely chopped onion in butter, and mix with the parsley. Fry the salmon steaks in a buttery pan. (They are naturally oily and need little extra fat). Allow them to cool, and when quite cold sprinkle them with salt and a little sugar, and brown them nicely on both sides under the grill. Sprinkle with onion and parsley, and serve with mayonnaise, potatoes and prunes.

LEFTOVERS: Mince and make into fish cakes, using cold cooked potatoes and a little egg to bind.

Stuffed Salmon Steaks

2 lbs. salmon	salt and a pinch of sugar	8 ozs. milk
4 ozs. butter	4 ozs. mushrooms or	chives
2 tablespoons flour	cooked prunes	water

Remove the skin and bone from the steaks, sprinkle them with salt and sugar and the finely chopped mushrooms or prunes. Roll them and tie them round with thread. Brown the butter in a frying pan, coat the steaks with flour and fry them a golden brown all over. Add a little water and allow them to poach until they are done, then add the milk. Remove the threads and serve with potatoes, prunes and pickles. Use the liquor as a sauce.

LEFTOVERS: Put the rolled steaks in a fireproof dish and cover with milk, mixed with a beaten egg. Bake, and serve hot. If the salmon is fresh, try grilling the skin and eating it with red pepper and lemon juice. This would make a good savoury.

Salmon Pie

flaky or short pastry

FOR STUFFING

3 eggs   *2 ozs. rice*   ½ *tablespoon butter*
5 ozs. cooked salmon   ½ *pint milk*   ½ *pint water*

Cook the rice, butter, milk and water together until the rice is done. Drain off any surplus moisture and cool. Prepare some pastry and roll it out into a square. Cover the middle with rice, then flakes of salmon, and lastly chopped hard-boiled eggs. Wet the edges of the pastry and pinch them together, points meeting in the middle, to form a smaller square. Brush over with milk and bake in a good oven. White fish may also be used, but it must be well seasoned with herbs, lemon, and anchovy.

LEFTOVERS: Cut into small pieces and eat, warmed, with hot bouillon.

Potato and Salmon Pudding

(Any other fish may be used with suitable flavouring to give it interest).

2 lbs. cooked potatoes   ½ *teaspoon salt*
8 ozs. fresh or tinned salmon   1 *teaspoon sugar*
3 eggs   4 *ozs. breadcrumbs*
1 pint milk   4 *ozs. melted butter*

Beat the eggs; add milk, seasoning and melted butter, and let the mixture stand for a little while. Break the salmon into pieces. Peel and cut the potatoes in slices, and arrange alternate layers of potato, salmon and egg mixture in a greased fireproof dish. The last layer must be potatoes. Sprinkle breadcrumbs on the top. Bake in the oven at 400° about 35 minutes or until the top is well browned and serve with melted butter and vinegar.

Any odd pieces of salmon may be used for this dish.

LEFTOVERS: Make into fish cakes and serve with a piquant tomato sauce.

Salted Salmon

1 *small salmon*   1 *teaspoon saltpetre*
2 *ozs. salt*   2 *tablespoons sugar*

Clean the salmon, and cut off the head and tail. Cut in half lengthwise and remove the backbone. Mix the salt, sugar, and saltpetre and rub the inside of the fish with it. Lay the halves of the fish in a bowl or wooden tub, with the insides together, and put a light weight on top. Next day the fish is ready. Serve cold, sliced with plenty of freshly ground black pepper and potatoes, or brown bread and butter.

Fish Jelly

2 lbs. salmon or any other fish	a piece of ginger
2 ozs. leaf gelatine	1 pint water
salt, sugar and peppercorns	1 bay leaf

FOR GARNISHING

hard-boiled eggs	cooked vegetables
parsley	2 whites of egg

Put the fish with the seasoning in cold water and bring it to the boil. Allow it to poach about twenty minutes. Lift out the fish, cut it in pieces and remove the head, tail and bones. When the liquid is nearly cold, strain it, stir in the whites of egg, and beat it on the fire until it begins to thicken. Remove it from the fire and stir in the gelatine, which has been melted in some of the liquid. Pour a little of the liquid into a mould, sprinkling it with chopped parsley. Arrange a layer of sliced hard-boiled egg, then put in the fish and pour in the rest of the liquid. Stand the mould in a cool place to set. Turn it out onto a dish, and serve with mayonnaise sauce, mustard, and vinegar.

LEFTOVERS: Break up the jelly with a silver fork, add cooked prawns and sliced tomato and serve on a bed of lettuce hearts.

Fish Pudding

1 lb. cooked white fish	salt, pepper and nutmeg
8 ozs. cream or evaporated milk	2 ozs. butter
2 tablespoons flour	2 eggs

Remove the skin and bones from the fish, and put it three times through a mincer or pound in a pestle and mortar. Add the beaten butter and whipped cream, yolks of eggs and seasoning. Beat the mixture until creamy, and add the whites of eggs whipped to a stiff froth. Grease a basin and sprinkle with breadcrumbs. Pour the mixture in and cover with greaseproof paper. Steam it for an hour. Turn out onto a dish and serve with mayonnaise.

LEFTOVERS: Cut the cold pudding in slices and serve with hollandaise sauce and sliced cucumber.

18

Meat, Poultry and Game

The country people in Finland eat large quantities of meat, pork and ham being especially useful, as their fat is a protection against the intense cold of the winter.

In the Autumn many farmers smoke two or more pigs. They build large wood fires in the bath house, close the ventilators, and hang the carcases in the smoke. For three or four days the fire is replenished, and then the sides of bacon are taken to the kitchen or storehouse and hung from hooks in the ceiling.

Game abounds in the forests of Northern Finland. In Autumn, the men form hunting parties and go out into the forest for days at a time to shoot birds. Sometimes the women go with them and pick mushrooms.

Game birds are seldom roasted, but fried in butter in large iron pots, turning them from time to time. The thickness of the iron gives a gentle and regular heat.

Many of the Finnish meat recipes make use of a little sugar. This can be omitted but it will be found that, used delicately, sugar does enhance the flavour of certain dishes in the same way as the pinch of salt used in making many English sweet dishes.

Finnish Roast Beef

4 lbs. sirloin or ribs of beef, boned and rolled
2 ozs. butter   1 egg   made mustard
salt and pepper   breadcrumbs   2 onions

Brown the sliced onion in butter in a roasting tin over the fire. Beat the beef well, and rub it with salt and pepper, mixed. Brown one side gently in the tin, then turn it, and coat the upper part with egg and breadcrumbs. Add a little boiling water and made mustard, and bake the joint in an oven pre-heated to about 400° for about an hour and forty minutes. Season and strain the gravy, and serve with mashed potato, carrot purée, or any other vegetable.

LEFTOVERS: Slice the meat and serve cold with mayonnaise.

Beef Stroganoff

2 lbs. tender lean beef, cut about half an inch thick
5 tablespoons butter   1 gill cream   half an onion
salt and pepper   2 tablespoons tomato sauce
2 tablespoons flour   1 tablespoon made mustard
water or stock   1 or 2 small salt gherkins

Wipe the beef with a damp cloth. Beat it and cut it in squares. Fry these in butter; sprinkle with salt, pepper, chopped onion and flour and allow them to brown a little while. Add the cream and a little water. Bring to the boil and turn into a saucepan. Rinse out the frying pan with water or stock and pour it over the beef. Simmer gently for about an hour. Before serving, season with tomato sauce, mustard and the gherkins cut in dice. Serve with sliced cucumber, or gherkins.

LEFTOVERS: Chop the meat finely, and serve it with a border of buttered rice and fried tomatoes.

Saturday Stew

¾ lb. shin of beef   1½ lbs. potatoes   salt and peppercorns
¾ lb. pork   1 onion   flour   water or stock

Cut the meat into squares about two inches big. Fry these together with the whole onion. When they are nicely browned, lift them out and put them into a saucepan. Work the flour into the fat which is left in the pan and stir in half a pint of water or stock gradually. Bring the sauce to the boil and pour it over the meat. Add the peeled potatoes, and enough liquid to cover. Season with salt and some peppercorns in a muslin bag. Simmer until the potatoes are cooked, then lift out the onion and the peppercorns and serve the stew hot.

LEFTOVERS: Chop the meat and potatoes and put them into a fireproof dish. Pour over them an egg beaten in a little milk, season and brown in the oven.

Beef in a Casserole

2 lbs. lean beef without bone		4 ozs. cream
salt and peppercorns	2 ozs. butter	sugar mustard
2 tablespoons flour	1 onion	water or stock

Wipe the beef with a damp cloth, and beat it well. Tie it round with string in order to keep it a good shape. Brown the whole onion in butter and then the beef, turning it on every side. After browning, sprinkle it with salt, pepper and flour. When the flour is brown, add a little water or stock, and then the cream. Allow the beef to simmer with the lid on. Before serving, lift the beef out and remove the string. Season the gravy with salt and mustard and beat it until creamy. If the sauce is not thick enough, add a teaspoonful of arrowroot mixed with water and bring to the boil. Serve with potatoes.

LEFTOVERS: Cut the beef in slices and fry these in butter. Serve with its own sauce, warmed up and sharpened with a spoonful of tomato ketchup.

Sour Beefsteak

2 lbs. buttock steak	salt and pepper	made mustard
2 pints ale or stout	2 ozs. butter	2 tablespoons flour
a trace of sugar		

Beat the steak well and put it to soak in the ale for two days. Lift it out, drain, sprinkle with salt and pepper and fry in butter until brown. Sprinkle the flour over the meat and brown once more. Add a little water and simmer for about two hours with the lid on. Season the gravy with salt, mustard and sugar, and strain. Serve with potatoes, fried cabbage, or salad.

LEFTOVERS: Use as a basis for curry.

Rolls of Beef

| 2 lbs. ribs of beef | 3 onions | 3 tablespoons flour |
| 4 ozs. butter | 5 peppercorns | 4 ozs. cream or evaporated milk |

Remove the bones from the meat, and cut it in slices about half an inch thick. Beat them, and score them across and across on both sides. Brown the onions in butter and remove them from the pan. Roll the slices of meat and brown them in the butter in which the onions have been fried. This must be smoking hot. Put the rolls of meat in an iron saucepan or casserole in layers, and sprinkle them with salt, pepper, onions and flour. Rinse out the frying pan with water, and pour it over the rolls. Allow them to simmer with the lid on until tender (about one hour).

If the meat becomes too dry, add a little boiling water. Lift out the rolls, add the cream to the gravy and strain it. Serve with potatoes and vegetables.

LEFTOVERS: Mince the meat and use it for rissoles.

Rolled Steaks of Beef

2 lbs. rump steak	8 ozs. fat bacon	2 tablespoons flour
salt and pepper	2 ozs. butter	parsley
1 gill cream or evaporated milk		mustard

Cut the steak in slices about three quarters of an inch thick and then into pieces about two and a half by four inches, and beat them well. Sprinkle each piece with salt and pepper, and lay on top of each a slice of bacon and a piece of parsley. Roll them up and tie. Fry them in butter till brown, sprinkle with flour and when the flour is brown, add first a little water and then the cream and mustard. Allow them to simmer about one hour. Remove the strings and serve with potatoes and vegetables.

LEFTOVERS: Mince and use for rissoles.

Lindstrom's Beefsteaks

| 1 lb. minced steak | 4 ozs. breadcrumbs | 3 eggs |
| 1 lb. cooked beetroot | salt and pepper | 2 ozs. butter |

Mince the beetroot, mix it with the steak and put them through a mincer. Add the eggs, breadcrumbs, salt and pepper and mix well. Shape into round flat cakes of equal size, about half an inch think, using two knives which have been dipped in cold water. Fry in butter. Add a little water, and allow them to simmer with the lid on about half an hour. Lift out the steaks and season the sauce. Serve with potatoes and vegetables.

LEFTOVERS: Mash and serve cold with mayonnaise sauce.

Sailor's Beefsteaks

2 lbs. buttock steak, cut in pieces about half an inch thick		
2 tablespoons butter	water or stock	salt and pepper
2 onions	¼ pint stout (this may be omitted)	1½ lbs. potatoes

Wipe the beef and cut it into neat round pieces. Beat them well. Then score them across and across on both sides with the blunt side of a knife. Brown the steaks with the onion, sliced. Arrange the meat and slices of potatoes in alternate layers in an iron pan. Sprinkle each layer with salt and pepper. Rinse out

the frying pan with a little water, and pour it over the meat. Add the stout and enough water to cover. Simmer with the lid on until the potatoes are cooked.

LEFTOVERS: Use for meat soup.

Fried Mutton

2 lbs. neck or breast of mutton   salt
6 peppercorns   2 eggs   breadcrumbs

Cut the mutton in pieces and put them into boiling salted water with the peppercorns. Simmer about an hour, and when the meat is tender lift it out and put it between two plates to cool. When cold, coat the pieces with beaten egg and breadcrumbs, and fry these golden-brown in smoking hot butter. Serve with hollandaise sauce, potatoes and vegetables.

LEFTOVERS: Serve the pieces cold with hard-boiled eggs and mayonnaise to which fresh chopped herbs have been added.

Mutton with Cabbage

2 lbs. scrag of mutton   1 small cabbage   2 ozs. butter
salt, sugar, peppercorns and mustard

Cut the mutton in pieces and brown these all over in the butter. Cut the cabbage in strips and arrange it in alternate layers with the meat in a heavy saucepan, sprinkling each layer with salt, peppercorns, sugar and made mustard. Rinse round the frying pan with a little water and pour it over the meat. Simmer for an hour and a half with the lid on, and serve with potatoes and mustard.

LEFTOVERS: Use as a salad with mayonnaise sauce.

Loin of Pork

2 lbs. tender loin of pork   salt   ginger   sugar
2 ozs. butter   4 ozs. cream or evaporated milk
2 tablespoons flour   juice of one lemon

Put the meat in a saucepan, and cover it with boiling water. Add the salt, sugar and a piece of ginger. Allow it to simmer with the lid on about an hour and a half, or until tender. Cut it in squares, and put it on a hot dish. Mix the butter and the flour, cook gently together and stir in the strained liquid. Boil for ten minutes, and just before serving stir in the cream.

LEFTOVERS: Chop the meat finely, re-heat, and serve with a border of rice, garnished with slices of lemon and hard-boiled egg.

Stuffed Loin of Pork

2½ lbs. loin of pork   1 small salted gherkin
2 ozs. cooked prunes   2 ozs. mushrooms   1 egg
2 ozs. cold cooked veal   2 ozs. breadcrumbs
2 ozs. cooked liver   salt and a trace of sugar

The bones must be removed from the meat, which should not be too fat. The loin of a small animal is preferable. Mince the cooked prunes, mushrooms, veal and liver and mix in the breadcrumbs, egg, salt and sugar. Spread the mixture over the open loin, roll it up and tie. Put a little water in a baking tin, and roast in a moderate oven (350°) about two hours, basting occasionally. Serve hot with peas, mustard, and pickles.

LEFTOVERS: Use the remains as a salad with mayonnaise.

Stewed Loin of Pork

2 lbs. boned loin of pork   4 ozs. cooked rice
4 ozs. cooked prunes   salt, made mustard, sugar

Stone and chop the prunes and mix them with the rice. Add mustard, sugar, salt and pepper. Spread the mixture over the loin, and roll and tie it round in several places. Cover it with boiling water, and allow it to simmer with the lid on for about an hour and a half. Serve with hollandaise sauce, potatoes, prunes or apple sauce, and mustard.

LEFTOVERS: Use as a salad with mayonnaise.

Pork Cutlets

2 lbs. loin cutlet of pork, cut about half an inch thick
2 ozs. cream or evaporated milk   2 ozs. butter   breadcrumbs
salt and pepper   1 medium sized onion   1 oz. flour

Cut the meat in pieces about three inches square. Beat them across on both sides with the flat of a knife. Fry the sliced onion golden-brown. Coat the cutlets with cream and breadcrumbs. Lift out the onion and brown the cutlets in butter. Put them onto a hot dish. Brown the flour in the butter, stir in boiling water gradually and a little cream to improve the colour. Season with salt and pepper. Pour the sauce over the cutlets, and sprinkle the slices of onion over them. Serve hot with potatoes.

LEFTOVERS: Chop the meat in pieces, fry, and mix with chopped fried bacon, tomatoes, potatoes, peppers, etc.

Rolled Pork

4 *lbs. lean loin of pork*   2 *teaspoons black pepper*   1 *lemon*
2 *tablespoons salt*   ½ *teaspoon ground ginger*   1 *tablespoon sugar*

Choose a piece from a small loin which has little fat. Mix the sugar, pepper and ginger with one tablespoonful of salt and rub the inside of the loin with it. Roll it up and tie tightly in several places. Put it in cold water with slices of lemon and a tablespoonful of salt. Bring it to the boil and simmer until tender, then put it in a large bowl. Strain over it the water in which it has been cooked. Allow it to cool and skim off the fat. Eat the pork sliced cold with potatoes, mustard and vinegar. The meat must be kept in the liquid and any which is left from a meal must be put back again. It will keep for weeks.

Stewed Veal

2 *lbs. loin or fillet of veal*   *salt and a very little sugar*
juice of two lemons   2 *tablespoons flour*
a piece of ginger

Beat the meat and tie it in a neat shape. Cover it with boiling water and add the lemon juice, ginger, salt and sugar. Simmer with the lid on for about two hours. Then lift out the meat, strain the liquid, add the flour mixed into a paste with the cold water, and allow it to boil for ten minutes. Pour the sauce over the veal, and serve hot with potatoes, vegetables and pickles.

LEFTOVERS: Mince the meat, mix it with the sauce and serve it with poached eggs and croutons of fried bread.

Fried Veal

2 *lbs. breast of veal*   4 *ozs. flour*   2 *eggs*   *breadcrumbs*
salt, pepper and a pinch of ground ginger   2 *ozs. butter*

Cut the meat in pieces and put it into hot salted water. Bring it to the boil and simmer about an hour and three quarters, then lift it out and put it to cool between two plates. Roll the pieces in flour mixed with the seasoning, and coat them with beaten egg and breadcrumbs. Fry rapidly in butter. Serve with currant sauce (page 72), potatoes and vegetables.

LEFTOVERS: Serve cold, as a salad with mayonnaise.

Rolled Steaks of Veal

2 lbs. of fleshy veal	salt	2 ozs. butter
8 ozs. prunes	2 eggs	8 ozs. cream
juice of one lemon	breadcrumbs	made mustard

Cut the meat in pieces about three quarters of an inch thick and three inches square. Beat them well. Lay a cooked stoned prune on each piece and sprinkle with salt and lemon juice. Roll up and tie. Coat the pieces with egg and breadcrumbs and fry them in butter till brown. Add a little water and allow them to simmer with the lid on for an hour and a half. When the rolls are cooked, lift them out, untie, and put them on a dish. Add the cream to the sauce, strain, and season with mustard.

LEFTOVERS: Serve cold, cut in slices with mayonnaise.

Liver in a Casserole

2 lbs. calf's liver	juice of one lemon	4 ozs. pork
2 ozs. butter water	salt and pepper	2 tablespoons flour

Cut the pork in thin strips and lard the liver, using a larding needle. Tie the liver round with string and fry it in butter until brown on every side. Sprinkle it with salt and pepper and pour into the pan enough water to prevent burning. Add the lemon juice and simmer with the lid on until done. Take out the liver and put it on a hot dish. Thicken the sauce with a teaspoonful of arrowroot mixed with cold water, stirred in and brought to the boil.

LEFTOVERS: Mince and use for stuffing tomatoes or potatoes.

Liver Pudding

¾ lb. calf's liver	1 egg salt	2 ozs. golden syrup
1 pint milk	onion	a pinch of herbs
¼ lb. rice	4 ozs. raisins	melted butter

Boil the rice in the milk until it is soft and then let it cool. Mince the liver and mix it with the cold rice. Add the onion which has been chopped and fried, the syrup, raisins, beaten egg and seasoning. Mix well and pour into a greased tin and bake about one and a half hours in a good oven (400°). Serve hot with melted butter.

LEFTOVERS: Cut the pudding in slices and fry.

Liver Roll

1 lb. calf's liver	½ teaspoon mustard
4 ozs. butter	1 onion 3 eggs salt
½ teaspoon ground cloves	8 ozs. fat pork
½ teaspoon ground ginger	¼ pint cream or evaporated milk
¼ teaspoon grated nutmeg	2 ozs. breadcrumbs

Put the liver through a mincer, add the breadcrumbs, eggs, cream, seasoning and chopped onion, which has been browned in butter.

Put the mixture through a sieve and beat it until smooth (or use the electric blender). Line a tin with thin slices of pork, pour the mixture in, and cover it with more slices of pork. (This roll is usually made in a long narrow tin with rather high sides, which makes a convenient shape for slicing). Cover the tin with greaseproof paper and stand it in boiling water. Cook for two hours, then move it from the fire, and let it cool as it stands. Serve cold, cut in slices, with potatoes, egg dishes, or bread and butter.

Blood Pudding

1 pint ox blood	2 ozs. butter	a pinch of herbs
2 pints stout	3 eggs	salt
2 onions	½ lb. rye flour	

Beat the yolks of egg and add the blood, well-beaten, chopped fried onions, rye flour and then the stout, very gradually, beating all the time. Leave it to stand for an hour, and add the seasoning and the beaten whites of egg. Grease a pudding basin, sprinkle it with breadcrumbs, and fill it three quarters full with the mixture. Cover with grease-proof paper. Stand it in a saucepan of boiling water, and cook for one and a half hours. Turn out and serve hot with melted butter and an acid jam or jelly.

LEFTOVERS: Cut the pudding in slices, fry these in butter, and serve them with Béchamel sauce.

Cold Tongue Steaks

1 ox tongue	juice of one lemon	salt and pepper
4 ozs. pork	4 ozs. butter	

Cook the tongue in boiling salted water and remove the skin. Cut the pork in slices and lard the tongue. Heat the butter in an iron pan and brown the tongue in it. Sprinkle with salt and pepper, add a little water and the juice of one lemon and simmer until tender. Make a sour-sweet sauce (page 71) using the gravy, and serve cut in slices with potatoes and vegetables.

LEFTOVERS: Serve cold with potato salad.

Tongue Salad

½ lb. cooked or smoked tongue   *mayonnaise sauce*
8 ozs. prunes

Cook the previously soaked prunes in a little water, stone them and mix them with slices of tongue and mayonnaise. Eat alone as a light dish or accompanied by vegetables.

LEFTOVERS: Arrange on a dish with hard-boiled eggs, sardines, etc., and use as hors d'oeuvre.

Kidney Salad

2 *sheep's kidneys*   2 *tomatoes*   *mayonnaise*
1 *gherkin*   8 *ozs. raisins*

Clean the kidneys, boil them in a little salted water and cut them in dice. Add the diced gherkin and tomato, and the raisins and seasoning. Mix with mayonnaise and serve with rolls and butter or with vegetables.

LEFTOVERS: Use for hors d'oeuvre as above, or lay spoonfuls of the mixture on crisp lettuce hearts.

Stewed Chickens

2 *small chickens*   1½ *ozs. sugar*   ¼ *pint cream or evaporated*
3 *ozs. butter*   7 *prunes*   *milk*
salt   *parsley*   ¼ *pint water*

Make the butter smoking hot in an iron pan, add the chopped parsley, and brown the chickens in it, turning them carefully. Cook the previously soaked prunes with the sugar and add them with their juice to the chickens. Sprinkle with salt, and simmer with the lid on for about an hour. Just before they are done add the cream. Before serving, cut the chickens in half along the breast bone and remove the trussing strings. Strain and season the sauce. Serve with potatoes and vegetables.

LEFTOVERS: Use to make a fricassee.

Duck with Apples

| 1 duck | salt | a trace of sugar | ¼ pint cream or |
| 1 lb. cooking apples | | 1½ tablespoons flour | evaporated milk |

The duck should be well hung. Stuff it with the peeled and cored apples cut in pieces, then fry it golden brown. Sprinkle it with salt, sugar and flour, and simmer until tender. Just before it is done, add the cream and allow it to boil. Season the gravy, skim off the fat and strain. Serve with potatoes and pickles.

LEFTOVERS: Curry and serve with rice.

Wild Duck with Sauerkraut

| 1 wild duck | 2 ozs. butter |
| 2 pints sauerkraut | salt, sugar and mustard |

Heat the butter in an iron pan, brown the duck and add the sauerkraut. Simmer with the lid on for about half an hour. Before serving, season with salt, a trace of sugar, and some made mustard.

LEFTOVERS: Use the meat for a salmi of duck.

Rabbit with Cabbage

| 1 rabbit cut in pieces | 4 ozs. butter | 6 peppercorns |
| a small cabbage | salt and sugar | |

Put half the butter in an iron saucepan and brown the cabbage, cut in strips. Brown the pieces of rabbit in a frying pan, using the rest of the butter. Sprinkle with salt, a trace of sugar, and pepper. Arrange the cabbage and rabbit in layers in the pan. Rinse the frying pan with a little water and pour it over. Simmer with the lid on about one and a half hours. Serve with potatoes.

LEFTOVERS: Use cold with fresh vegetables and mayonnaise.

Luncheon and Supper Dishes

Sausages are made at home on the farms in Finland. They are made with a mixture of meats and the lungs and hearts of calves are often included. Sometimes the sausages are hung in strings from the roof of the storehouse, or they are kept in tubs of salted water.

In the streets of the bigger towns there are stalls where small boiled sausages are sold. Each sausage is laid on a piece of paper with a large dab of mustard. Tearing off a corner of the paper to hold the sausage, people walk along the street dipping it in mustard and eating as they go. These sausages are very popular at night when the restaurants are closed, especially with students and late workers.

Barley Sausage

½ *lb. whole barley*	*salt and a trace of sugar*	2 *onions*
2 *pints milk*	½ *lb. raisins*	3 *ozs. butter*

Wash the barley and cook it in milk with the raisins and seasoning, and the onion fried golden brown in butter. When tender, fill a sausage skin loosely, using a mincer with a nozzle. Make the sausage about one and a half inches thick, and tie at both ends. The sausage must be laid on straw and baked. The straw which is wrapped round bottles may be used, but it must be well brushed. Bake about an hour in a moderate oven (350°). Cool and fry it, sliced, in butter. Serve hot with melted butter.

Liver Sausage

1 *pig's liver*	1 *lb. loin of pork*	*salt and pepper*
6 *ozs. fat pork*		1 *onion*

Bring the liver to the boil in salted water, and put it through a sieve. Add the meat and the fat pork, cut in dice. Stir in grated onion, salt and pepper. Fill a pig's bladder very tightly with the mixture. Cook half an hour in a little salted water. Serve cold in slices with bread and butter, or egg dishes.

Rice and Liver Sausages

| 8 ozs. rice | 8 ozs. calf's liver | 1 oz. syrup | salt |
| 2 pints milk | 6 ozs. raisins | 4 ozs. butter | 1 onion |

Put the liver through a mincer, and cook the rice with the milk. Allow it to cool, and mix it with the liver. Add the chopped onions fried in butter, raisins, syrup and salt. Mix well, and fill a sausage skin loosely, twisting the skin between each sausage. Put the sausages in a little salted water, bring to the boil and simmer for one hour. Before serving, fry them in butter, and sprinkle with melted butter.

Tomato Eggs

| 6 large tomatoes | 2 ozs. cream (or sour | salt and pepper |
| 6 eggs | cream) | butter |

Cut a slice from the top of each tomato, and scoop out the inside. Break an egg into each tomato. Sprinkle with salt and pepper, and cover with cream. Replace the slice of tomato. Make some butter smoking hot in a fireproof dish, arrange the tomatoes on it and keep them on the heat for about ten minutes. They can be finished under the grill.

Baked Eggs

| ¼ pint cream or milk | 2 ozs. grated cheese |
| 6 eggs | 4 ozs. chopped bacon |

Pour the cream onto a fireproof dish, and break the eggs into it. Sprinkle with cheese and bacon, and put it in the oven. Bake until the whites of eggs are set. Serve hot with mustard, caper, or hollandaise sauce.

LEFTOVERS: Chop and heat in cheese sauce. Serve on hot buttered toast.

Sardine Eggs

| 6 eggs | mustard and pepper | lard for frying |
| 3 sardines | 4 ozs. breadcrumbs | |

Hard-boil five of the eggs. Remove the shells, and cut them in half lengthwise. Scoop out the yolks, and mix them with pounded boned sardine and seasoning. Fill half the eggs, and press them together again. Coat them with beaten egg and breadcrumbs, and fry golden brown. Serve with mayonnaise or mustard sauce.

LEFTOVERS: Cut the eggs in slices, and use for salad.

Bacon Pancakes

2 eggs	½ pint milk	4 ozs. flour
4 ozs. bacon (in rashers)	4 ozs. water	butter for frying

Cut the bacon in squares and fry it lightly. Beat the eggs and add milk, water, flour and bacon, making sure that there are no lumps. Fry thin pancakes on one side only, roll up and serve very hot with castor sugar and salt. (The sugar is an acquired taste and may be omitted. Try it at least once, though, it is surprisingly good).

LEFTOVERS: Cut in slices and eat with soup.

Stuffed Pancakes

Using the same mixture as before, fry thick pancakes and when they are nearly done, spread over them a layer of hot vegetables mixed with butter and salt. Spinach, mushrooms, celery, cauliflower or tomato are particularly good. Cold vegetables may be warmed up. Delicious combinations can be made with mixtures of vegetables, or by adding raisins, prawns, fried onion, chutney or fried pimentos.

Blood Pancakes

These are considered a great delicacy in Finland, and are perhaps an acquired taste, but one well worth acquiring.

½ pint blood (calf's or pig's blood is best)		
½ pint milk or stout	5 tablespoons rye flour	half an onion
3 tablespoons barley flour	1 tablespoon salt	butter for frying
4 tablespoons dripping or lard	pepper	1 egg ½ teaspoon herbs

Put the blood through a sieve and beat it well. Stir in the milk or stout and the flour, beating all the time. Brown the sliced onion in butter and add it with the seasoning and beaten egg to the mixture. Fry thin pancakes in an omelet pan, and serve with melted butter and an acid jelly or jam.

LEFTOVERS: Cut in slices and fry. Serve with cream sauce.

Stuffed Beetroot

6 small fresh beetroots	2 ozs. tinned salmon	1 oz. butter
1 hard-boiled egg	1 oz. smoked tongue	parsley
sugar, pepper and breadcrumbs		

Bake the beetroots in the oven, peel them, cut a slice from the top of each and scoop out the centres. Mix the chopped eggs, salmon, tongue, parsley and seasoning well together. Stuff the beetroots with the mixture, adding a little of the chopped centres, and cover each with the slice that was removed. Put them in a greased baking dish and sprinkle with breadcrumbs. Brown them under the grill. Serve with cream sauce (page 71) and potatoes.

LEFTOVERS: Use for a rich vegetable soup.

Stuffed Cabbage

1 cabbage	4 ozs. breadcrumbs	2 ozs. butter
½ lb. minced steak	4 ozs. rice, cooked	1 egg
salt, sugar and mustard		1 tablespoon brown sugar

Cook the cabbage in fast boiling, salted water, only until the leaves become soft enough to bend. Strip off the leaves, setting aside the largest. Mix the rice with the beef. Add the salt, a trace of sugar, mustard, beaten egg, and breadcrumbs. Moisten with a little milk or water, add the smallest leaves of the cabbage, chopped, and mix well. Lay as much on each leaf as may conveniently be wrapped round, and tie with thread. Brown the rolls in butter and put them in a greased baking tin, sprinkling them with sugar and salt. When all the rolls are browned, rinse the frying pan with a little water, pour it over them and put the tin in the oven for about three quarters of an hour. Strain and season the gravy, remove the strings, and serve with potatoes and vegetables.

LEFTOVERS: Chop the rolls and make them into rissoles, or use them to fill omelets.

Stuffed Carrots

12 carrots	2 ozs. cream	sugar and salt
8 ozs. breadcrumbs	10 almonds	2 ozs. butter
2 eggs	4 ozs. rice, cooked	

Clean the carrots and cook them in water. Cut them in half lengthwise and hollow them. Mix the rice with the breadcrumbs, seasoning, cream, chopped almonds, eggs, salt and very little sugar. Mix well, adding a little of the inside of the carrot. Stuff the carrots and tie the halves together. Brown the carrots in butter and sprinkle them with brown sugar. Serve with mayonnaise and potatoes.

LEFTOVERS: Make into carrot soup.

Stuffed Celeriac

4 celeriac roots	3 ozs. ham	1½ ozs. sugar
6 cooked prunes	2 ozs. rice, cooked	2 eggs
3 ozs. breadcrumbs	salt	

Wash the celeriac and cook until tender. Cut them in half and hollow them out. Mix the rice with the chopped ham and hard-boiled eggs. Add the chopped prunes, which have been slightly salted and mix in some of the scooped-out inside of the celeriac. Fill the hollowed roots with the mixture and tie the halves together. Coat with beaten egg and breadcrumbs and fry in butter. Serve with currant sauce (page 72) and potatoes or pickles.

LEFTOVERS: Use as a salad with mayonnaise.

Stuffed Cucumber

3 cucumbers	4 ozs. cooked rice	salt and sugar
3 eggs	breadcrumbs	4 ozs. butter
8 ozs. cooked salmon, fresh or tinned		

Peel the cucumbers and cook them in boiling salted water. Slice them in half lengthwise and remove the seeds. Mix two chopped hard-boiled eggs with the rice and add the salt, a trace of sugar and the salmon, mashed with a fork. Mix well and fill the hollowed cucumbers. Tie the halves together, coat them with egg and breadcrumbs and fry in butter. Serve with currant sauce (page 72) potatoes and pickles.

LEFTOVERS: Use as salad with mayonnaise.

Potato and Bacon Pudding

| 2 lbs. cooked potatoes | ½ pint milk | salt and pepper |
| 10 ozs. bacon | 3 eggs | |

Cut the potatoes and the bacon into dice, and mix together. Put them into a greased fireproof dish. Pour over them the eggs, beaten with the milk and seasoned. Bake in the oven and serve hot with melted butter and vegetables.

LEFTOVERS: Use for filling pancakes.

Sauerkraut Pudding

1 *pint sauerkraut (or one tin)*　　4 *ozs. cooked prunes*
½ *lb. pork or Frankfurt sausages*　*small meat balls*
2 *tablespoons breadcrumbs*　　　2 *ozs. butter*
2 *ozs. golden syrup*

Fry the meat balls in butter and cut each sausage into three pieces. Mix all together with the sauerkraut in a greased fireproof dish, sprinkle with breadcrumbs and bake one hour. Serve with toast.

LEFTOVERS: Heat and serve on hot buttered toast.

Cabbage Pie

a portion of flaky or short pastry　1½ *teaspoons brown sugar*
some melted butter　　½ *pint water or stock*　　1 *cabbage*
2 *ozs. butter*　　　1 *tablespoon salt*　1 *tablespoon vinegar*

Brown the butter and fry the chopped cabbage in it. Add the water or stock and simmer in a covered pan until the cabbage is cooked. Drain off any surplus moisture, add the seasoning and let it cool. Roll out half the pastry into a square and lay it on a baking sheet, piling the mixture in the middle so that one inch from the edge all round is left free. Roll out the other half into a slightly smaller square, lay it on top and fold the underneath edge over it. Press all round and mark with the back of a knife. Bake it in a good oven (450°) and serve hot with melted butter. This may also be left open like a jam tart and covered with lattice-work strips of pastry. In this case less pastry is needed and also a shorter time to bake.

LEFTOVERS: Cut up into small pieces, warm and eat with hot soup.

Savoury Slices

Cheese Slices

6 *slices of white bread*   2 *ozs. butter*   *chopped parsley*
2 *ozs. grated cheese*   *cooked beetroot*

Cut the crusts from the slices. Beat the butter to a cream, and spread it on the bread. Cover with cheese and sprinkle with chopped beetroot and parsley.

Brown Cheese Slices

6 *slices of brown bread*   2 *ozs. butter*
6 *thin slices of cheese*   *French mustard, radish and chives*

Cut the crust from the bread. Beat the butter to a cream, flavouring it with French mustard. Spread it on the slices, covering each with a piece of cheese trimmed to fit. Sprinkle with chopped radish and chives.

Cold Meat Slices

6 *slices of white bread*   6 *thin slices of cold meat*
2 *ozs. butter*   *a little red currant jam or jelly*

Remove the crust from the slices and spread them with creamed butter. Lay a piece of meat on each slice and decorate with a lattice-work of red currant jelly. The meat may also be cut in strips or minced, and flavoured in any other way.

Ham Slices

6 *slices of white bread*   2 *ozs. butter*
3 *ozs. lean ham*   6 *prunes*

Mince the ham and mix it with creamed butter. Cover the toast with this mixture and decorate with chopped prunes.

Sausage Slices

6 *slices of white bread*   2 *ozs. butter*
2 *ozs. sliced cooked sausage*   2 *ozs. cooked prunes*

Remove the crusts from the slices and spread them with creamed butter. Chop the sausage, pound it into a paste with a wooden spoon and spread it on the bread. Stone the prunes, and lay a prune on each sandwich, or cover half of each sandwich with sausage and half with chopped prunes.

Tomato Slices

6 slices of white bread   2 ozs. butter   1 cooked mushroom
1 hard-boiled white of egg   6 small tomatoes   salt and pepper

Cut rounds from slices of white bread, using a pastry cutter.
Spread them with creamed butter, mixed with chopped mushroom.   Cut the tomatoes crosswise so that they fall open in
four sections, and put a tomato on each slice.   On the centre of
each tomato put a little chopped white of egg, and sprinkle with
salt and pepper.

Giant Sandwich

1 brown loaf   cold veal   cooked mushrooms
3 ozs. butter   cucumber   parsley   salt and pepper

Cut the crust from the loaf, slice it and spread with creamed
butter.   Arrange between layers of buttered bread alternately
sliced cucumber, mushroom, chopped veal (or any other
combination) seasoning as you go with salt and pepper.   Press
firmly together, sprinkle with chopped parsley, chill and slice
downwards across the layers with a sharp knife.

Rainbow Sandwich

1 white loaf   grated cheese   chopped prunes
1 brown loaf   sausage   salmon
4 ozs. butter   mustard   salt and pepper

Remove the crusts from the loaves and cut them horizontally
in thin slices.   Spread the slices on both sides with creamed
butter.   Using brown and white alternately, arrange them in
layers, spread with cheese, mustard, sausage, salmon and prunes.
Fold in a damp towel, put a light weight on top and chill.   The
following day, cut in slices downwards so that the sandwiches
are striped.   Any other fillings may be used, such as raw herring,
sliced onion, chopped hard-boiled egg, mayonnaise, etc.

This would be useful for picnics or late suppers, as it can be
prepared the day before.

Anchovy Egg Toast

4 slices of toast   8 fillets of anchovy
4 eggs   12 capers

Cover each slice of toast with a fried egg, decorated with two
fillets of anchovy, and three capers.   Serve hot with caper or
mustard sauce.

Chicken Toast

6 slices of toast cooked peas mayonnaise sauce
remains of cooked chicken chopped prunes

Butter each slice of toast thinly and top it with chopped chicken, surrounded with peas and chopped prunes. Decorate with rosettes of mayonnaise.

Fish Toast

6 slices of toast horse-radish mayonnaise sauce
cooked fish chopped prunes salt and pepper

Put a little chopped fish in the centre of each slice and surround with prunes. Decorate with grated horse-radish and mayonnaise tinted with a little tomato sauce. Sprinkle with salt and pepper.

Mushroom Toast

¼ lb. cooked mushrooms or a small tin
6 slices of toast chives 1 tablespoon butter
6 scrambled eggs mayonnaise salt and pepper

Arrange the mushrooms in the centre of each slice, surround them with scrambled egg, and sprinkled with chopped chives. Garnish with mayonnaise and sprinkle with salt and freshly grated black pepper.

Savoury Egg Toast

4 slices of toast butter
4 eggs salt, pepper and made mustard
4 slices of meat roll or cold sausage

Cover each piece of toast with a slice of meat roll seasoned with mustard, and lay on top of it a fried egg. Sprinkle with salt and pepper, and serve hot with mustard or hollandaise sauce.

Grilled Cheese

8 ozs. gruyère cheese 1 egg 4 ozs. breadcrumbs

Cut the cheese in thin slices, coat these with beaten egg and breadcrumbs, and brown them under the grill, on both sides. Serve hot with brown bread, toast or biscuits.

Vegetables

With the exception of potatoes, the peasants in Finland eat hardly any vegetables.

During the winter and early spring fresh vegetables are almost unobtainable and their place used to be taken by dried and salted ones. There are now plentiful supplies of tinned and frozen fruit and vegetables.

Finland rejoices in a wealth of mushrooms. In the autumn, whole families make expeditions into the forest to gather them. Often they take a horse and cart loaded with great baskets and everyone, including the children, helps to fill these from smaller baskets which they carry. About twenty five different kinds of mushrooms are used but the favourites are lamb's mushroom, short and white with a flesh like chicken, and furry mushrooms, which are covered with a soft golden brown down. A small bright orange mushroom is pickled in vinegar and looks very pretty on the table. These must be carefully picked into separate baskets, as they are spoilt when they are broken.

Mushrooms must be cleaned at once. Sometimes they are skinned, and the stalks thrown away in the forest, but if the pick is very large, they are brought home and cleaned at night. After a big supper, the whole family gathers in the bath house and works together, stripping and sorting the mushrooms. Water is boiled in a large cauldron and when, after long boiling, their bitterness is gone, the mushrooms are drained and salted in wooden tubs for use through the winter.

In springtime, a dark brown crinkled mushroom grows in the forest. These are threaded on strings and hung up to dry.

Fried Cabbage

1 cabbage   2 tablespoons brown sugar
2 ozs. butter   1 tablespoon vinegar

Cut the cabbage in slices. Brown the butter in an iron pan and fry the cabbage. When it is well browned add the sugar and the vinegar and allow it to simmer under a lid. If it is too dry add a little water and stir. Serve hot with mutton or pork.

LEFTOVERS: Use for cabbage pudding or soup.

Fried Spanish Onions

4 large Spanish onions   breadcrumbs
salt and a trace of sugar   4 ozs. butter

Boil the onions in salted water and then cut them in thick slices. Sprinkle with salt and sugar and coat them with egg and breadcrumbs. Fry them in butter. Serve with currant sauce (page 72) and pickles.

LEFTOVERS: Serve chopped with herrings, or as a salad with mayonnaise.

Fried Carrots

2 lbs. small carrots   breadcrumbs   salt
1 egg   2 ozs. butter

Clean the carrots, and cook them in a little salted water. Allow them to cool, coat them in egg and breadcrumbs and fry them golden brown in butter. Serve with meat.

LEFTOVERS: Mince or chop the carrots and make them into balls.

Baked Cauliflower

1 cauliflower   1 tablespoon breadcrumbs   salt
2 ozs. butter   1 tablespoon grated cheese   1 egg

Clean the cauliflower, remove the leaves and allow it to soak for several hours in cold water. Then coat it with beaten egg and sprinkle with cheese and breadcrumbs. Melt the butter in a baking tin and bake the cauliflower in a moderate oven until tender, basting frequently. Serve with meat dishes or separately as a lunch or supper dish.

LEFTOVERS: Warm and serve with melted butter as a vegetable.

Pea and Carrot Stew

| 1 *pint dried peas* | 1 *pint water* | *salt and sugar* |
| 1 *lb. carrots* | 2 *ozs. flour* | 2 *ozs. butter* |

Wash the peas and put them to soak overnight in the water in which they are to be cooked. Clean the carrots, cut them in pieces and boil them with the peas. When they are cooked add the flour which has been mixed with a little water and boil for ten munutes. Then season, add the butter and serve hot with fish or meat.

LEFTOVERS: Use as a basis for rissoles.

Potato Balls

| 2 *lbs. freshly cooked potatoes* | 8 *ozs. milk* | 2 *eggs* |
| 2 *ozs. butter* | *salt and pepper* | 4 *ozs. bacon* |

Mash the potatoes and add the butter, boiling milk, salt and pepper. Beat well until they are creamy. When cool, add the beaten eggs and seasoning and make balls, pressing a hole in each. Fill the hole with diced bacon and cover it over. Put the balls into boiling water and cook them until they rise to the top. Serve hot with meat and fish dishes. They are especially good with veal.

LEFTOVERS: Coat the balls with egg and breadcrumbs and fry, or mash them and fill a fireproof dish. Cover them with grated cheese and bake.

Cabbage Balls

| *half a cabbage* | 2 *eggs* | *a pinch of herbs* |
| 4 *ozs. breadcrumbs* | *salt and sugar* | 2 *ozs. butter* |

Boil the cabbage, and when cooked chop it very finely. Drain it carefully and add the breadcrumbs, eggs and seasoning. Mix well and form into small balls. Fry them golden brown in butter and serve with onion sauce (page 73) or pickles.

LEFTOVERS: Chop and fry with bacon.

41

Celeriac Balls

| 1½ lbs. celeriac | 4 ozs. breadcrumbs | salt and pepper |
| 2 eggs | 10 almonds | 2 ozs. butter |

Clean and boil the celeriac. Mince, and add the eggs, bread-crumbs, chopped blanched almonds, salt and pepper and mix until smooth. Form into small balls and fry. Serve with mush-room sauce.

LEFTOVERS: Use for puddings, or as dumplings with soup.

Carrot Cakes

| 1 lb. carrots | 2 eggs | salt, sugar and nutmeg |
| 8 ozs. rice | 4 ozs. flour | breadcrumbs | 2 ozs. butter |

Clean, boil and mince the carrots. Steam the rice and mix it with the carrots; add one egg, salt, sugar and nutmeg. Mix well and form into flat cakes, using the blades of two knives. Coat with flour, egg and breadcrumbs, and fry them in butter. Serve with sardine sauce (page 72) and potatoes.

LEFTOVERS: Mash the cakes, add a little cream and use as a vegetable.

Pea Cakes

1 lb. dried peas	a pinch of herbs	2 ozs. butter
2 eggs	2 ozs. flour	breadcrumbs
salt, a pinch of sugar and mustard		

Boil the peas until they are soft enough to go through a sieve. Add one egg, flour, herbs, salt, sugar and made mustard. Mix well and if too soft, add some more flour. Form into cakes with two knives. Coat with egg and breadcrumbs and brown them in butter. Serve with caper sauce, potatoes and pickles.

LEFTOVERS: Use with herrings and mayonnaise as a salad.

Spinach Cakes

| ½ lb. spinach | 2 eggs | 8 ozs. breadcrumbs | salt and sugar |
| 4 ozs. macaroni | 4 ozs. flour | water | 4 ozs. butter |

Put the washed spinach into hot water and bring it to the boil. Drain well and chop finely. Cook the macaroni in boiling salted water, chop it and mix it with the spinach. Add one egg, half the breadcrumbs and the salt and sugar. Mix well and, using the blades of two knives, form into flat cakes. Coat them with

flour and then with egg and breadcrumbs. Fry them in butter and serve with apple sauce, potatoes and pickles.

LEFTOVERS: Slice the spinach cakes and warm them. Pour a little melted butter over them and use as accompaniment to cold meat.

Rice Cakes

4 *ozs. rice*	2 *ozs. butter*	*salt, a trace of sugar and*
1 *pint milk*	*breadcrumbs*	*ground cloves* 1 *egg*

Cook the rice in milk. Allow it to cool and mix with one egg, salt, a trace of sugar and a little ground cloves. Shape with the blade of a knife into flat cakes, coat them with egg and breadcrumbs and fry them in butter. Serve with mustard sauce.

LEFTOVERS: Break up the rice cakes, add a little milk and beaten egg, cover with grated cheese and tomato sauce and brown in the oven or under the grill.

Chestnut Cakes

1 *lb. chestnuts*	*salt and pepper*	*breadcrumbs*
2 *eggs*	2 *ozs. butter*	

Cook the chestnuts in their skins. Peel them and put them through a sieve. Mix in the eggs and seasoning, shape into flat cakes and egg and breadcrumb them. Fry them golden brown and serve with apple sauce and vegetables.

LEFTOVERS: Use with mayonnaise as a salad.

Potato Pudding

2 *lbs. freshly cooked potatoes*		3 *tablespoons melted butter*
1 *cup milk*	1 *tablespoon salt*	2 *tablespoons breadcrumbs*
1 *egg*		

Put the potatoes through a masher while still hot and stir in the butter and boiling milk. Add the beaten egg and seasoning and pour the mixture into a greased fireproof dish. Sprinkle it with breadcrumbs and bake in a hot oven for about an hour.

LEFTOVERS: Shape into cakes, egg and breadcrumb and fry.

Carrot Pudding

1½ *lbs. carrots*	8 *ozs. breadcrumbs*	*nutmeg and a very little*
water and salt	½ *pint milk*	*sugar*
3 *tablespoons melted butter*		2 *eggs*

Clean the carrots and cook them in salted water. Put them through a sieve or mash them carefully. Mix them with the other ingredients, pour into a greased fireproof dish and bake for about an hour.

LEFTOVERS: Sieve, or blend in an electric mixer and use for soup.

Rice and Carrot Pudding

4 ozs. rice   1 lb. carrots   salt, nutmeg and pepper
1 pint milk   2 ozs. butter   3 eggs   breadcrumbs

Wash the rice, cook it in the milk and let it cool. Clean, boil and mince the carrots and mix them with the rice. Beat in the eggs and seasoning. Pour into a greased dish and sprinkle with breadcrumbs. Put dabs of butter on the top and bake about an hour. Serve with melted butter and pickles.

LEFTOVERS: Slice the pudding and fry it, or eat it with soup.

Cauliflower Pudding

1 small cauliflower   4 ozs. flour   salt and sugar
2 ozs. cream or   2 ozs. butter   5 almonds
   evaporated milk   3 eggs

Cut the cauliflower in pieces and cook it in boiling salted water until very tender. Mash it and mix it with the finely chopped almonds, and beat in the eggs, cream and seasoning. Bake it in a fireproof dish sprinkled with breadcrumbs and pieces of butter, and serve with tomato sauce. The pudding may also be steamed.

LEFTOVERS: Slice and fry, or break it up with a fork and mix it with hot cheese sauce.

Spinach Pudding

1 lb. fresh spinach (or a small packet of frozen)
4 ozs. rice   1 pint milk   2 ozs. breadcrumbs
½ pint water   2 eggs   1 tablespoon sugar
1 tablespoon melted butter   1 tablespoon salt

Prepare the spinach carefully, washing the leaves and tearing off the stalks, and bring it to the boil in salted water. Boil for from 5 to 15 minutes according to the age of the spinach, drain and chop coarsely. If frozen spinach is used just bring to the boil, drain and chop. Cook the rice in the milk and water and let it cool. Add the spinach, butter, breadcrumbs, beaten yolks of egg and seasoning and lastly, the whites of the eggs beaten to a stiff froth. Pour the mixture into a deep greased fireproof dish and stand it in a tin of water. Bake it for about an hour in a moderate oven.

LEFTOVERS: Cut in slices and fry, or warm and serve as an accompaniment to soup.

Tomato Pudding

| 1 *lb. tomatoes* | 4 *ozs. breadcrumbs* | 2 *ozs. butter* |
| 3 *eggs* | 2 *ozs. cream* | *salt and pepper* |

Cut the tomatoes in half and put them through a mincer, removing the pips. Add the beaten butter, whipped cream, yolks of eggs, breadcrumbs and seasoning. Beat until creamy, and add lastly the whites of eggs whipped to a stiff froth. Steam in a pudding basin for about an hour and a half. Turn out and serve with potatoes, salted fish and mayonnaise.

LEFTOVERS: Cover with mayonnaise and serve cold, or use as a filling for omelets.

Onion Salad

| 6 *Spanish onions* | *parsley* | *water* |
| *French dressing* | *salt* | |

Boil the onions in salted water, peel, drain and cut them in slices. Arrange them in a basin, pour French dressing over them and garnish with parsley. Serve with hot fish or meat.

Vegetable Salad

10 *small carrots*	10 *runner beans*	10 *Brussels sprouts*
10 *shallots*	1 *small cooked cauliflower*	*mayonnaise*
10 *small Jerusalem artichokes*		

Clean the carrots and artichokes and cook them until soft. Cook together the Brussels sprouts, sliced beans and shallots. Mix all the vegetables and cover them with mayonnaise. Serve with cold meat and egg dishes.

LEFTOVERS: Use for hors d'oeuvre with sardines, hard-boiled eggs, etc.

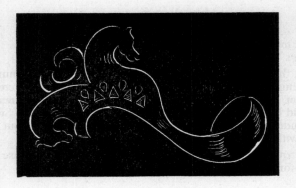

Puddings

Puddings are not traditionally Finnish and are eaten only by educated people. The peasants eat instead sweet soups and porridges. Baked pancakes are used a great deal and are often called Tuesday food. Pea soup is usually eaten before pancakes.

Baked Nut Pudding

5 eggs	2 ozs. flour
6 ozs. sugar	8 ozs. chopped walnuts

Beat the yolks of eggs and sugar until creamy and stir in the flour and chopped walnuts. Add the whites of eggs beaten to a stiff froth. Bake in a fireproof dish which has been greased and sprinkled with breadcrumbs. Turn out and serve hot with jam and vanilla sauce.

LEFTOVERS: Cut in slices and use instead of cake.

Chestnut Pudding

6 ozs. chestnuts	2 ozs. butter	2 ozs. almonds
1 pint milk	5 eggs	caramel made from 4 ozs.
a vanilla pod	4 ozs. sugar	sugar

Boil the chestnuts for half an hour and, after removing the inner and outer skins, simmer them with milk and the vanilla pod until they are soft and broken. Lift out the vanilla pod, drain the chestnuts and put them through a sieve. Add the butter, yolks of eggs, sugar and the peeled and chopped almonds.

46

Fold in the whites of eggs, beaten to a stiff froth. Melt the sugar for the caramel, and stir it over the fire until it is brown and syrupy. Pour it into the basin in which the pudding is to be cooked. Put in the chestnut mixture, cover it with greaseproof paper and steam for two hours. Turn out onto a dish, and serve hot with jam or fruit sauce.

LEFTOVERS: Mash the pudding, mix it with cream, and serve cold with strawberry jam.

Steamed Walnut Pudding

6 ozs. sugar   6 ozs. chopped walnuts
5 eggs   4 ozs. breadcrumbs

Beat the yolks of eggs and sugar until they are stiff and add the nuts, breadcrumbs and the whites of egg, beaten to a stiff froth. Grease a basin and sprinkle it with breadcrumbs. Steam the pudding in it for two hours. Turn out, and serve hot with berry juice sauce (page 74) or whipped cream.

Fruit Pudding

4 ozs. apples   1 cup water   8 ozs. cream
4 ozs. prunes   8 ozs. sugar   6 ozs. sugar for caramel
2 ozs. dried apricots 4 eggs

Wash the dried fruit and soak it for several hours with one cup of warm water to which three ounces of sugar have been added. Lift out the dried fruit and cook the peeled and cored apples in the juice. When the apples are ready lift them out and cook the prunes and apricots in the same syrup. Heat six ounces of sugar until it becomes a dark brown syrup and line a warmed mould with it. Arrange the fruit round the inside of the mould. Beat the eggs, add the whipped cream and pour into the mould. Add the remains of the fruit, stand the mould in a bain-marie and allow it to cook from one to two hours, or steam it for two hours. Turn out and serve hot with its own syrup, or with vanilla sauce.

LEFTOVERS: Eat cold with custard or cream.

Epicure Pudding

1 tablespoon butter   1½ pints milk
2 tablespoons flour   2 eggs   jam

Cook the butter and flour together in a saucepan, add the boiling milk gradually and allow it to boil a little while. Let the mixture cool, stirring from time to time. Add the beaten yolks of egg and then the whites, beaten to a stiff froth. Grease a fireproof dish and spread a layer of jam on the bottom, fill it with the mixture and bake golden brown. Serve hot with cream.

LEFTOVERS: Slice, and use as a nursery trifle with cream and jam.

Orange Rice

2 ozs. rice   2 eggs   2 ozs. sugar
2 ozs. butter   ¾ pint milk   2 small oranges
a few drops of almond essence

Wash the rice and cook it with the milk and butter in a double saucepan. When the rice is soft, lift the inner saucepan onto the fire, add the sugar and grated rinds of the oranges and let it boil a few minutes, stirring all the time. Remove it from the fire to cool, add the lemon juice and beaten yolks of egg, a few drops of almond essence and then the whites of egg beaten to a stiff froth. Put the pudding into a basin which has been greased and sprinkled with breadcrumbs and steam for two hours. Turn out onto a dish and serve with berry juice sauce (page 74) or vanilla custard.

LEFTOVERS: Mix the pudding with whipped cream and serve with jam.

Meringue Rice

1 portion of orange   4 whites of egg   4 ozs. almonds
    rice (see above)   8 ozs. icing sugar   4 ozs. cooking
                                                chocolate

Pile the orange rice high in a fireproof dish. Beat the whites of egg and add, gradually, the sugar and chopped almonds. Cover the rice with some of the mixture and decorate it with the rest, using an icing syringe. Put it in the oven to brown slightly. Melt the chocolate with a little water, and pour it over the rice so that it runs down in streaks. Serve with jam and whipped cream.

LEFTOVERS: Cover with grated chocolate and serve with cream.

Baked Almond Apples

1 lb. apples   4 ozs. breadcrumbs   4 ozs. sugar
2 ozs. almonds   1 egg   2 ozs. flour   2 ozs. butter

Peel and core the apples. Blanch and chop the almonds and mix them with half the sugar. Fill the apples with this mixture. Beat the eggs and add the rest of the sugar. Dip the apples in flour, coat them with the egg beaten with a little sugar and then breadcrumbs. Melt the butter in a fireproof dish in the oven and turn the apples in it until they are brown all over. Bake them in a moderate oven from half to three quarters of an hour. Serve with vanilla sauce, and jam.

LEFTOVERS: Put through a sieve or cream in the electric blender and serve cold.

Apple and Rusk Pudding

1 *pint milk*	10 *rusks*
1 *egg*	½ *pint apple purée*

Beat the egg, add the milk and soak the rusks in it for an hour. Mash them with a spoon and put half the mixture in a greased fireproof dish. Cover with a layer of apple purée and then a second layer of rusk mixture. Bake golden brown and serve hot with cream or vanilla sauce.

LEFTOVERS: Serve cold with vanilla sauce.

Fried Jam Sandwiches

10 *slices of white bread (stale bread will do)*		
¼ *pint milk*	4 *ozs. jam*	1 *tablespoon sugar*
1 *egg*	¼ *pint cream*	*butter for frying*

Dip the slices of bread in beaten egg and milk and fry them golden brown. Make them into sandwiches with jam. Beat the cream, add the sugar, and decorate the sandwiches with it.

LEFTOVERS: When they have stood for a time these sandwiches become tough and little can be done with them except to feed hungry birds.

Golden Brown Sandwiches

12 *slices of white bread (stale bread can be used)*	
2 *ozs. jam, or berry purée*	4 *ozs. baked breadcrumbs*
1 *egg*	*cream and sugar*

Cut the crust from the slices and make sandwiches with jam or purée. Coat them with beaten egg and breadcrumbs and fry golden brown. Serve hot with sugar and cream.

LEFTOVERS: Serve cold for tea.

Raisin Twins

10 *slices of white bread (stale or fresh)*
4 *ozs. suet*   2 *ozs. sugar*   ½ *pint milk*
3 *ozs. almonds*   4 *ozs. raisins*   2 *eggs*

Chop the suet finely and add the peeled and chopped almonds and sugar. Dip the slices of bread in beaten egg and milk. Make sandwiches of the almond mixture and sprinkle them with raisins. Arrange them in a fireproof dish and bake. Serve hot with whipped cream or vanilla sauce.

LEFTOVERS: Serve cold with cream.

Prune Dumplings

1 *lb. cooked prunes*   1 *egg*   *salt*   8 *ozs. flour*
4 *ozs. sugar*   *water*   2 *ozs. butter*

Stone the prunes. Beat the egg with two tablespoonfuls of sugar, and add two tablespoonfuls of water and the flour. Knead the dough well until it no longer clings to the fingers, then roll it out about half an inch thick and cut it into rounds about three inches across. Put a prune in the centre of each, fold over, and pinch the edges together. Put the prune balls into boiling water, and allow them to boil ten minutes. Dip them in melted butter, sprinkle with sugar and serve hot with vanilla, chocolate or coffee sauce.

LEFTOVERS: Use at tea, or serve with coffee, instead of cake.

Prune Doughnut

1 *or 2 yolks of egg*   ¼ *pint milk*   ½ *oz. yeast*
1 *oz. butter*   8 *ozs. flour*   *a pinch of salt*
½ *lb. prunes, cooked with 4 ozs. sugar*
lard for frying   ½ *pint water*

Beat the yolks of egg and butter till creamy and add the milk, salt and yeast, made into a paste with a little milk. Stir in the flour and knead until the dough does not cling to the fingers. Stand it in a warm place until it has risen. (This usually takes about an hour). Then knead again, roll it out rather thin and cut it in rounds, stuffing them with prunes in the same way as prune dumplings. Let them rise again and fry them in boiling fat. Drain well and sprinkle with castor sugar. Serve hot with vanilla, chocolate or coffee sauce.

LEFTOVERS: Use instead of cake for afternoon tea.

Finnish Pastry

1 egg	¼ pint water	½ teaspoon soda	8 ozs. flour
1 desertspoon brandy		¼ teaspoon alum	4 ozs. butter

Beat the egg and add the water, brandy, soda, alum and flour, and mix until smooth. Roll it out on a floured board about half an inch thick and cover half the pastry with dabs of butter. (If the butter is salt it must be washed in warm water and dried carefully in a cloth). Then fold the paste in half, and stand in a cool place for fifteen minutes. Repeat this process three or four times until all the butter has been used. The pastry must be turned each time that the rolling pin is passed over it, so that it is rolled each time from a different direction. This makes a fine flaky pastry but if a quicker recipe is wanted, the butter may be rubbed into the flour in the ordinary way, and the egg, brandy and water mixed in together. The pastry must be baked in a quick oven.

Apple Roll

a portion of Finnish pastry (see preceding recipe)		1 egg
8 ozs. apple purée	4 ozs. almonds	8 ozs. breadcrumbs
4 ozs. raisins	4 ozs. sugar	grated rind of one lemon

Butter a piece of greaseproof paper and roll out the pastry on it as thin as possible. Cover it with apple purée, sprinkle with raisins, peeled and chopped almonds, breadcrumbs, lemon rind and sugar. Roll it up in the same way as a Swiss roll, turn it onto a baking sheet and coat with beaten egg. Bake and serve hot with vanilla or chocolate sauce.

LEFTOVERS: Decorate with whipped cream and use as a cake.

Pancake

1 pint milk	1 tablespoon melted butter	4 ozs. flour
2 eggs	2 tablespoons sugar	butter for frying

In Finland these pancakes are made in a pan divided into seven small hollows and so they are easily turned and keep a better shape. An ordinary pan may of course be used instead.

Beat the eggs and sugar and add the flour, melted butter and milk gradually. Leave it to stand for two hours and if it is then too thick add a little milk. Melt the butter in a pan and fry thin pancakes, browning them on both sides. Put them on a dish, which should be kept hot over a saucepan of boiling water. Serve immediately with castor sugar and slices of lemon, or jam.

LEFTOVERS: Warm up and eat with fruit soup, or bake with jam spread between, and beaten egg and milk poured over.

Jam and Cream Pancake

Pancake mixture   ¼ pint cream   butter for frying
8 ozs. jam   2 ozs. sugar

Fry thin pancakes in an omelet pan. When the first pancake is ready, turn it out onto a warmed dish and cover it with a layer of jam. Repeat this until all the mixture is used. Allow the pancakes to cool a little, whip the cream, add the sugar and cover the pancakes with it. Serve immediately.

LEFTOVERS: Use in the same way as cold pancake.

Baked Pancake with Cream

8 ozs. cream or evaporated milk   1 oz. melted butter
2 eggs   2 tablespoons sugar   ½ teaspoon powdered
4 ozs. flour   ¼ teaspoon cinnamon   cardamom

Beat the eggs and sugar well and add the melted butter, seasoning, cream and flour. Pour the mixture into a baking tin which has been greased and sprinkled with flour. Bake in a moderate oven about an hour. Lift onto a hot dish and serve with sugar and jam or slices of lemon.

LEFTOVERS: Use in the same way as cold pancake.

Layer Pancake

½ pint milk   8 ozs. flour   ¼ pint cream or evaporated milk
4 eggs   a pinch of salt   4 tablespoons sugar

Beat the eggs and sugar well, add the beaten cream, flour and, lastly, the milk. Bake as above and serve hot with jam and sugar. When the pancake is cut it will be seen that it has formed two layers, the softer one on top.

LEFTOVERS: Use in the same way as cold pancake.

Potato Pancake

6 ozs. flour   2 tablespoons sugar   6 ozs. cooked potatoes
8 ozs. jam   6 ozs. butter   ½ pint cream or evaporated milk

Mash the potatoes and mix them with the flour. Rub in the butter and mix smoothly. On a floured board roll out to a thickness of about half an inch. Using the lid of a saucepan, cut rounds about six inches across. Bake them and arrange them on a dish in layers with jam between. Cover the pancake with sweetened whipped cream and serve hot.

LEFTOVERS: Slice and fry and serve with castor sugar and slices of lemon.

Cold Sweets

Apricot Cream

8 ozs. dried apricots   1 pint water   1 pint milk
4 ozs. cornflour   4 ozs. sugar

Soak the apricots overnight in the water in which they are to be cooked. Bring them to the boil with sugar and simmer until they are soft, but not broken. Lift them out with a perforated spoon into a crystal dish. Mix the cornflour into a paste with cold milk, add the juice from the apricots and, stirring all the time, bring it to the boil. Pour the mixture over the apricots and stir gently. Serve cold with cream or vanilla sauce.

LEFTOVERS: Rub through a sieve and mix with a little cream (or use the electric blender) and serve decorated with almonds and angelica.

Coffee Cream

4 eggs   6 ozs. sugar   a few drops of vanilla essence
3 tablespoons strong black coffee, or 1 tablespoon coffee essence
6 ozs. butter

If the butter is salt wash it well, and beat it to a cream. Beat the eggs, coffee and sugar in a saucepan until the mixture is thick. Remove it from the fire and beat until cold. Mix in the butter and beat until it is nearly white. Pour the cream into a basin and chill. Serve with biscuits.

LEFTOVERS: Cut sponge cake in layers, spread coffee cream between, and use as a cake.

Prune Cream

½ lb. prunes   2 ozs. berry juice   1 teaspoon arrowroot
1 pint water   2 ozs. sugar

Wash the prunes and soak them overnight in the water in which they are to be cooked. Bring them to the boil with the sugar and simmer till quite tender but not broken. Lift them out with a perforated spoon into a crystal dish. Colour the liquid with berry juice and add the arrowroot which has been made into a paste with cold water. Bring it to the boil and pour it over the prunes, mixing well. Serve cold with whipped cream.

LEFTOVERS: Use for stuffing fish, etc.

Rainbow Cream

1½ pints milk	1 oz. sugar	different colourings
3 ozs. cornflour	1 egg	

Heat the milk and add the sugar and cornflour mixed into a paste with cold water. Bring it to the boil, remove it from the fire and add the beaten egg. Continue to beat until it is quite cold. Divide it into as many parts as you have colours, and tint each. Then mix all together carefully so that the colours form streaks. Pour into a crystal dish and chill. Serve with whipped cream or vanilla sauce, and jam.

LEFTOVERS: Flavour the cream with coffee and serve it in custard glasses, decorated with whipped cream.

Almond Jelly

½ pint cream	a vanilla pod	½ oz. powdered gelatine
3 ozs. almonds	2 ozs. sugar	2 ozs. water

Peel and chop the almonds and bring them to the boil with the cream, vanilla and sugar, keeping the lid on the pan. Remove it from the fire and add the leaf gelatine which has been melted in hot water. Lift out the vanilla pod and stir until the mixture cools. Pour it into a mould which has been rinsed out with cold water and put it to chill. Turn out and serve with jam.

LEFTOVERS: Serve with sliced oranges or stewed apricots.

Berry Juice Jelly

3 yolks of egg	8 ozs. sugar	½ oz. powdered gelatine
1 tablespoon flour	¼ pint cream	4 ozs. berry juice (rasberry, red currant, cherry etc.)

Beat the yolks of egg, flour, sugar and the ¼ pint of cream on the fire until they thicken. Remove the saucepan from the fire and beat until the mixture is cool. Melt the gelatine in hot berry juice, cool it and add it to the egg mixture. Whip the rest of the cream to a stiff froth, and fold it in. Pour the mixture into a rinsed jelly mould. Chill. Turn out onto a dish and serve with waffles, or biscuits and jam.

LEFTOVERS: Break up with a silver fork and serve with cream.

Tea Jelly

½ pint cream	6 ozs. sugar	½ pint strong tea
2 yolks of egg	¾ oz. powdered gelatine	

Mix the tea, and half the cream. Beat the yolks of eggs and sugar, and mix them with the tea. Beat over the fire until the mixture thickens and add the leaf gelatine which has been melted in a small quantity of hot water. Lift it from the fire to cool and add the rest of the cream, beaten. Pour the mixture into a rinsed mould, and put it to chill. Turn out, and serve with jam and almond juice.

LEFTOVERS: Use as filling for sponge cake sandwiches.

Berry Milk Jelly

1½ pints milk	grated rind of half a lemon	2 ozs. water
5 ozs. sugar	1 oz. powdered gelatine	

½ pint berry juice (raspberry, red currant, cherry, loganberry etc.)

Bring the milk, sugar and lemon rind to the boil and then allow them to cool. Melt the gelatine in hot water and add the berry juice. When both mixtures are cool, fold them together, and pour into a mould which has been rinsed out with cold water. Set it to chill. Turn it out into a dish and serve with cream or jam.

LEFTOVERS: Break up the jelly with a fork, mix it with strawberry jam and serve in custard glasses.

Prune Cream Jelly

½ lb. prunes	½ pint cream	½ oz. powdered gelatine
½ pint water	4 ozs. sugar	

Wash and boil the prunes. When they are tender remove the stones, and chop the prunes quite fine, mixing in the juice in which they have been cooked. Beat the cream quite stiff and add the sugar. Melt the gelatine in hot water, let it cool a little and stir in the prunes. Whip the cream, fold it in to the prune jelly, pour into a crystal dish and allow it to set. Serve cold.

LEFTOVERS: Break up with a fork, stir in more cream and sprinkle with chopped toasted nuts.

Cold Brandy Cream

This should be made with arrack, but this is difficult to get and very expensive, and brandy will do quite well instead.

3 eggs	½ pint cream	¾ oz. powdered gelatine
2 ozs. sugar	a vanilla pod	1 to 2 tablespoons brandy

Beat in a saucepan the yolks of egg, sugar, cream, vanilla and gelatine, which has been melted in a little hot water. When the mixture has thickened but not boiled, remove the saucepan from the fire, and beat until cool. Add the brandy and the whites of

egg, beaten to a stiff froth. Pour the pudding into a crystal basin to set. Decorate it with jam and whipped cream.

LEFTOVERS: Break it up with a fork, and serve piled on top of sliced oranges.

Foam Ice Cream

1 *pint of berry juice*   4 *whites of egg*   4 *ozs. castor sugar*

Put the berry juice into the freezing tray until it begins to stiffen. Beat the whites of egg and add the sugar. When the juice is half frozen stir in the whites of egg gradually, and then let the mixture freeze, stirring from time to time. Serve with whipped cream or vanilla sauce, and biscuits.

LEFTOVERS: Pile up in glasses and serve decorated with whipped cream, fruit and chopped nuts.

Iced Fruit

3 *lbs. fruit* (*apples, pears, bananas, white grapes, plums, pineapple*
    etc.)   2 *lemons*   *praliné almonds*
           8 *ozs. sugar*   *whipped cream*

Peel the larger fruits and cut them in pieces. (The small ones may be left whole). Dip each piece of fruit in lemon juice, and then in sugar. Lay them in the freezing tray, and when they are really cold but not hard, turn out onto a crystal dish and sprinkle with praliné almonds. Serve with whipped cream.

LEFTOVERS: Sieve, or whip in the electric blender, and use for fruit jelly.

Orange Charlotte

¾ *oz. powdered gelatine*   8 *ozs. sugar*   2 *whites of egg*
juice of one lemon   ½ *pint water*   *grated rind and*
                                          juice of one orange

FOR DECORATION: *quarters of orange*

Melt the gelatine in half pint of water. Stir in sugar, lemon and orange juice, and the grated rind of orange. Set it to chill and then beat until frothy. Add the stiffly whipped whites of egg, and beat the mixture until it is firm. Decorate a mould with quarters of orange and fill it with the mixture. Chill, and then turn out and serve cold.

LEFTOVERS: Serve with fruit salad.

Chocolate Rice

4 ozs. rice   ½ pint cream   2 ozs. chocolate
½ pint boiling water   1 oz. sugar

Wash the rice well and throw it into the boiling water. After a quarter of an hour add the cream, sugar and chocolate broken into small pieces. Simmer until the rice is quite creamy. Then cool, stirring occasionally. Turn out on a dish and serve with cream and grated chocolate.

LEFTOVERS: Cover with meringue and put in the oven to brown lightly.

Lemon Rice

8 ozs. rice   water   2 lemons
8 ozs. sugar

Boil the rice, drain, and pour cold water over it until the water is clear. Boil together four ounces of water, the sugar, lemon juice, and the grated rind of lemon until they thicken, and mix the syrup with rice. Simmer in a double saucepan for an hour. Remove to cool and turn out onto a crystal dish. Serve with whipped cream, stewed fruit, etc.

LEFTOVERS: Mix with cream or milk, and serve with jam and biscuits.

Jam Snow

6 ozs. jam   2 ozs. sugar   3 whites of egg

Beat the whites of egg to a stiff froth, add gradually the sugar and jam, and beat until the snow is white and fluffy. Turn onto a dish and serve with biscuits.

LEFTOVERS: Use to decorate a baked pudding.

Sweet Soups and Porridges

After meat, the country people eat large bowls of sweet soup, usually made with berries or dried fruit. Porridges of various kinds are used too, the favourite being rice. Curiously enough oatmeal is disliked by most of the peasants. As milk is very plentiful, junkets and various curds are eaten a great deal in summer.

A fruit soup makes an economical and unusual sweet course. In Finland it is generally eaten with sweet bread. We have no exact substitute for Finnish bread, but sponge cakes or sweet biscuits may well be used instead. A large bowl of soup with a silver ladle, a small bowl before each person, and a basket lined with an embroidered cloth and filled with sliced cake, rusks, or biscuits, would give a fresh aspect to the end of a meal.

Fruit porridges should be served in a deep dish, and eaten with plenty of milk and sugar. Children enjoy them, and will drink in this way a great deal of milk which might not otherwise tempt them.

Hot Apple Soup

1 lb. fresh apples or ½ lb. dried apples   1 oz. chopped almonds
2½ pints water   2 ozs. butter   sugar   4 ozs. rice

Peel and core the apples and cut them in pieces. Wash and half cook the rice in two and a half pints of water. Add the apples. When both are cooked, but not broken, add the butter and sugar, and pour the soup into a bowl. Sprinkle it with almonds, and serve hot with almond biscuits and whipped cream.

LEFTOVERS: Use for rice and apple porridge.

Cold Apple Soup

1 lb. fresh apples or 8 ozs. dried apples
2½ pints water   4 ozs. sugar
1 tablespoon cornflour   a stick of cinnamon

Peel and core the apples and cut them in pieces. Put them in cold water with the sugar and cinnamon, and bring to the boil. Simmer them until they are soft but not broken. (If dried apples are used, wash and soak them for several hours in the water in which they are to be cooked, and then use them in the same way as fresh apples). Lift out the pieces of apple with a perforated spoon and put them into a bowl; then mix into the apple juice the cornflour, made into a smooth paste with cold water. Allow it to boil a few minutes, lift out the cinnamon and then pour the

liquid over the apples.   Sprinkle with almonds and serve cold
with rusks or sweet biscuits.

LEFTOVERS: Thicken with apple purée, and eat with whipped
cream.

Apricot Soup

½ lb. dried apricots or 1 lb. tinned apricots
2½ pints water   1½ tablespoons cornflour
4 ozs. sugar   1 tablespoon chopped almonds

Make in the same way as cold apple soup and serve with
apricot jam and whipped cream.

LEFTOVERS: Thicken with cream or evaporated milk, add a
teaspoon of powdered gelatine dissolved in hot water, and freeze.

Bread Soup

½ lb. stale bread   2 pints water   3 ozs. sugar
½ pint purée of any sharp flavoured fruit

Soak the bread in the water until it is soft.   Stir in the fruit
purée and put the mixture through a sieve.   Boil, and sweeten
the soup.   If necessary, flavour it with a little lemon juice.   Serve
hot with almond dumplings (page 69) and whipped cream.

LEFTOVERS: Use for bread porridge.

Cherry Soup

1½ lbs. fresh cherries or 1 lb. tinned or bottled cherries
2½ pints water   1 tablespoon flour   2 ozs. chopped almonds
2 ozs. butter   2 ozs. sugar

Before cooking, crush the cherries and the stones, then simmer
them for about half an hour with the water and put them through
a sieve.   Cook the butter and flour together, add the sieved cherries
gradually, boil ten minutes, flavour, and mix in the almonds.
Serve hot with biscuits and whipped cream.

LEFTOVERS: Use as a sauce with a steamed pudding.

Hot Berry Soup

1½ *lbs. fresh berries or 1 lb. tinned (blackberry, raspberry, red*
    currants etc.)   1½ *tablespoons flour*
2 *ozs. sugar (only if fresh berries are used)*   2 *pints water*
1 *oz. chopped almonds with the skin left on*   2 *ozs. butter*

Put the berries in cold water and bring them to the boil.
Let them simmer until tender, then put them through a sieve.
(If tinned berries are used, sieve them without cooking). Cook
the butter and flour together, and add the hot soup gradually.
Sweeten, and allow it to boil ten minutes. Serve hot, sprinkled
with almonds, and eat with whipped cream and biscuits.

LEFTOVERS: Thicken with arrowroot and eat as a porridge
with milk.

Cold Berry Soup

1½ *lbs. fresh berries or 1 lb. tinned (blackberry, raspberry, red*
    currant etc.)   2 *ozs. sugar (only if fresh berries are used)*
2 *pints water*   1 *tablespoon chopped almonds*
1½ *tablespoons cornflour*   *the rind of one lemon*

Cook and sieve the berries in the same way as for hot berry
soup. Re-heat, and before boiling stir in the cornflour made into
a paste with cold water. Sweeten, and let it boil a few minutes.
Pour the soup into a bowl, and before serving sprinkle with
chopped almonds and grated lemon rind. Serve cold with rusks,
milk bread, or rice porridge.

LEFTOVERS: Use as sauce with steamed puddings.

Fig Soup

½ *lb. dried figs*   2 *ozs. sugar*   2 *ozs. butter*
2½ *pints water*   *half a lemon*   1 *tablespoon flour*
2 *ozs. raisins*

Soak the figs overnight in two and a half pints of water, cut
them in pieces, add lemon juice, simmer until they are tender,
and put them through a sieve. Cook the butter and flour well
together, add the soup gradually, and boil together with the
raisins and fine strips of lemon rind. Simmer until the lemon
rind is soft. Serve hot with raisin dumplings (page 69) or almond
dumplings (page 69).

LEFTOVERS: Use as a sauce for steamed puddings.

Lemon Soup

2 *lemons*	3 *ozs. sugar*	1 *tablespoon cornflour*
2½ *pints water*	2 *ozs. almonds*	

Heat the lemon juice, sugar, water and finely peeled lemon rinds and just before they come to the boil, add the cornflour mixed into a paste with cold water. Boil a few minutes. Let it cool, stir in the chopped almonds, and serve cold with almond biscuits and whipped cream.

LEFTOVERS: Use as a sauce or pour over cold stewed prunes or figs.

Orange Soup

5 *oranges*	4 *ozs. sugar*
2½ *pints water*	1 *tablespoon cornflour*
1 *tablespoon red berry juice or a few drops of cochineal*	

Bring to the boil the juice of three oranges, water, sugar and berry juice or cochineal. Just before boiling add the cornflour made into a paste with cold water. Let it boil a few minutes, then pour it into a bowl to cool. Just before serving float two peeled, sliced oranges on the soup, and serve with whipped cream and rice dumplings (page 69).

LEFTOVERS: Use as a sauce.

Pear Soup

1 *lb. fresh pears or ½ lb. dried pears*

2½ *pints water*	2 *ozs. sugar*	1 *tablespoon red berry juice*
1½ *tablespoons flour*	2 *ozs. butter*	*or some cochineal*

a vanilla pod or a few drops of vanilla essence

Peel and core the pears and cut them in pieces. (Dried pears must be soaked overnight in the water in which they are to be cooked). Cook the pears with sugar and vanilla, and berry juice or cochineal colouring. When the pears are cooked but not broken, add the butter, and the cornflour mixed into a paste with cold water. Remove the vanilla pod and serve the soup hot with whipped cream and biscuits.

LEFTOVERS: Serve chilled with sliced stewed pears in it.

Rhubarb Soup

1 *lb. rhubarb*	2 *ozs. sugar*	1 *tablespoon chopped almonds*
2½ *pints water*	1½ *tablespoons cornflour*	*a stick of cinnamon*

Peel the rhubarb and cut it in pieces about one inch long. Simmer these gently with a little water until soft, and then put them through a sieve. Remove the soup from the fire and mix in the cornflour made into a paste with cold water. Flavour the soup with sugar and cinnamon and boil for a few minutes, then pour it into a bowl to cool. Lift out the cinnamon. Serve the soup cold, sprinkled with chopped almonds, and eat with raisin or rice dumplings (page 69).

LEFTOVERS: Thicken with arrowroot, stir in a little cream and serve well beaten in glasses.

Rowan Soup

½ *lb. rowan berries, picked after a frosty night*

2½ *pints water*	4 *ozs. sugar*	2 *ozs. chopped almonds*
4 *ozs. raisins*	1 *tablespoon sago*	½ *tablespoon cornflour*

Cook the berries in water till soft, then put them through a sieve. Pour them back into the saucepan with the sago, sugar and raisins. Add the cornflour mixed into a paste with cold water, and boil it for a few minutes. Pour into a basin to cool and sprinkle with almonds. Serve with meringue dumplings (page 69).

LEFTOVERS: Use as a sauce, or to flavour puddings.

Milk Soups

Chocolate Soup

2 *pints milk*	2 *ozs. sugar*	1 *teaspoon arrowroot*
1½ *tablespoons unsweetened cocoa*		*a few drops of vanilla essence*

Bring the milk to the boil and beat in the sugar and the cocoa made into a paste with hot water. Let the mixture boil for a few minutes. Remove the saucepan from the fire and add the arrowroot made into a paste with cold water. Boil a few minutes longer. Serve hot with almond cakes, or meringue dumplings (page 69).

The soup may also be thickened by using yolks of egg instead of arrowroot. The yolks should be beaten in a bowl and the soup poured onto them while boiling, stirring all the time.

LEFTOVERS: Use as a sauce with steamed puddings.

Curd Soup

2 *pints milk*   2 *teaspoons vinegar*   *sugar*

Bring the milk to the boil and add the vinegar, so that the milk curdles. Allow it to boil ten minutes, then sweeten to taste. Serve hot with squares of cinnamon toast.

LEFTOVERS: Chill and sprinkle with cinnamon.

Egg Soup

2 *pints milk*   1½ *ozs. sugar*
2 *yolks of egg*   *grated rind of half a lemon*

Bring the milk to the boil and add the sugar and grated lemon rind. Beat the yolks of egg in a bowl and stir in the boiling soup. Serve hot with meringue dumplings (page 69) or almond pastries.

LEFTOVERS: Use for making custard or mixing puddings.

Jam Milk

1½ *pints milk*   1 *yolk of egg*   3 *ozs. jam*

Bring the milk to the boil. Beat the yolks of egg in a bowl and add the milk, beating all the time. Just before serving, stir in the jam. Serve with biscuits or almond dumplings (page 69).

LEFTOVERS: Use to moisten trifle, bread and butter pudding, or other sweets.

Special Oatmeal Soup

In Finland this soup is eaten a great deal, and is sometimes called health soup.

2 *ozs. rolled oats*   1 *teaspoon salt*   1 *tablespoon sugar*
½ *pint milk*   10 *prunes*   1 *oz. chopped almonds or*
                                               2 *drops of almond essence*

Wash the prunes in warm water and put them to soak overnight with sugar and half a pint of water. Boil them until soft. Bring the oats to the boil in one pint of water, and simmer them until they are cooked. Beat in the boiling milk and bring the mixture to the boil once more. Add the salt, the prunes with their juice, and the chopped almonds or almond essence. Serve hot.

LEFTOVERS: Lift out the prunes and use them for stuffing fish. The liquid will make a stock for soups or porridges.

Oatmeal Soup with Wine

Make in the same way as special oatmeal soup. When it is ready, stir in a gill of cream, half a tablespoonful of butter and a glass of white wine.

Simple Oatmeal Soup

2 *ozs. sugar*	2 *ozs. rolled oats*	*rind of half a lemon*
1 *oz. butter*	*a pinch of salt*	4 *ozs. raisins*
10 *cooked prunes with their juice*		

Boil the oats in two pints of water and put them through a sieve. Add the butter, rind of lemon, raisins, sugar and prunes with their juice. Serve hot with almonds or grated lemon peel and biscuits.

LEFTOVERS: Use for flavouring, or eat with stewed prunes.

Sago Soup

1½ *pints milk*	1 *yolk of egg*	2 *ozs. sago or tapioca*
1 *oz. butter*	*a pinch of salt*	*sugar and cinnamon to taste*

Add to the boiling milk the washed sago or tapioca and simmer until it is quite clear. Stir in the butter, cinnamon, salt and sugar, and bring the soup to the boil. Beat the yolks of egg in a bowl, and stir in the boiling soup. Serve hot with almond biscuits or meringue dumplings (page 69).

LEFTOVERS: Add chopped almonds, thicken with arrowroot and set in a mould, decorating with jam.

Semolina Soup

2 *pints milk*	1 *oz. butter*
2 *ozs. semolina*	*cinnamon, sugar and salt*

Bring the milk to the boil and beat in the semolina. Let it boil for half an hour. Add butter, flavour and serve hot with jam meringues, or whipped cream.

LEFTOVERS: Thicken with arrowroot, add cream and lemon and eat hot with cinnamon and sugar.

Snowball Milk

2 pints milk　　2 eggs　　1 oz. castor sugar
1 teaspoon arrowroot　　a few drops almond essence
½ teaspoon flour　　½ teaspoon ground cinnamon

Beat the whites of egg to a stiff froth, add the sugar and vanilla and beat until shining. Fold in the cornflour and almond essence. Drop spoonfuls of the mixture onto boiling milk. Simmer until the snowballs are firm, then lift them out with a perforated spoon. Beat the yolks of egg, flour, and cinnamon in a bowl and add some milk, beating all the time. Continue until all the milk has been added. Float the snowballs on the liquid and serve hot with almond cakes.

LEFTOVERS: Beat the soup until the balls are mixed in and use for a sauce or for flavouring porridges.

Stout Soup

1 pint stout　　a few cardamoms　　2 tablespoons flour
1½ pints milk　　2 ozs. sugar or golden syrup
½ tablespoon chopped dried orange peel　　a piece of ginger

Cook the stout and milk separately. Add to the stout the orange peel, cardamoms, ginger and sugar or syrup. When it is boiling, skim well. Add to the boiling milk the flour, made into a paste with cold milk, and allow it to boil ten minutes. Then mix all together. Serve hot with croutons of fried bread, or with cream cheese.

LEFTOVERS: Use to moisten a rich fruit cake.

Sweet Porridges

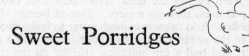

Apricot Porridge

6 ozs. dried apricots　　2 ozs. sugar
4 ozs. semolina　　vanilla essence

Let the apricots soak overnight in two pints of water. Add the sugar and bring them to the boil. Beat the semolina in gradually. Simmer the porridge for half an hour. Flavour with vanilla and serve cold with milk and sugar.

LEFTOVERS: Serve with whipped cream, or beat with cream and chopped almonds and eat with biscuits.

Apple Porridge

1 *lb. fresh, or ½ lb. dried apples*   2 *ozs. cornflour*
2 *ozs. sugar*   *a cinnamon stick*

Peel and core the apples (if dried apples are used, soak them overnight in the water in which they are to be cooked). Simmer the apples with cinnamon and sugar until they are soft but not broken. Remove the cinnamon, add the cornflour made into a paste with cold water, and let it boil a few minutes. Serve cold with milk and sugar.

LEFTOVERS: Put in a fireproof dish, cover with breadcrumbs, dabs of butter, brown sugar and a sprinkling of cinnamon, and bake.

Barley Porridge

1 *pint milk*   1 *oz. butter*   *salt and cinnamon*
2 *ozs. patent barley*   1 *oz. almonds*

Bring the milk to the boil and beat in the barley and chopped almonds. Simmer half an hour, beating all the time. Stir in butter and salt; sprinkle before serving with cinnamon. Serve hot with milk and sugar or jam.

LEFTOVERS: Add the beaten yolk of an egg and bake. Serve with jam.

Berry Porridge

2 *lbs. fresh berries, or a tin of fruit*
2 *ozs. cornflour*   2 *ozs. sugar*

If fresh berries are used, cook them with two pints of water and put them through a sieve. Tinned berries should be sieved uncooked. Add to them enough water to make two pints of liquid. Stir in the sugar and the cornflour, made into a paste with cold water, and boil a few minutes, stirring all the time. Turn out onto a dish to cool. Serve cold with milk and sugar.

LEFTOVERS: Decorate with jam and cream and serve in custard glasses.

Butter Porridge

2 *pints milk*   5 *ozs. flour*
2 *ozs. butter*   *salt and sugar*

Melt the butter in a saucepan, add the flour and cook them ten minutes without allowing them to brown. Beat in the boiling milk gradually, and then boil for ten minutes. Flavour, and serve hot with milk and honey.

LEFTOVERS: Thin with top of the milk, flavour with marmalade, lemon, etc., and use as a sauce.

Chocolate Porridge

2 *pints milk*   3 *ozs. cornflour*   *vanilla essence*
1½ *tablespoons powdered chocolate*   2 *ozs. sugar*

Bring the milk to the boil, flavour with vanilla, stir in the chocolate and sugar and the cornflour, made into a paste with cold milk. Boil the porridge for ten minutes. Turn onto a dish and serve cold with milk and sugar.

LEFTOVERS: Pile up in glasses and decorate with whipped cream.

Egg Porridge

2 *pints milk*   2 *yolks of egg*
2 *ozs. cornflour*   *sugar, salt, and the rind of one lemon*

Bring the milk to the boil and add the cornflour mixed into a paste with cold water. Boil the porridge for half an hour. Stir in a pinch of salt, sugar to taste and grated lemon rind. Remove the porridge from the fire and mix in the beaten yolks of egg. Beat well and serve hot with milk, sugar or jam.

LEFTOVERS: Eat cold with large spoonfuls of jam stirred into it in whirls.

Flour Porridge

2 *pints milk*   *vanilla flavouring*
3 *ozs. flour*   2 *ozs. sugar*

Bring the milk and vanilla to the boil and beat in the flour made into a paste with cold water. Boil the porridge for twenty minutes, and pour it onto a dish. Serve hot with milk, and sugar or jam.

LEFTOVERS: Eat with stewed fruit.

Golden Crust Porridge

Remains of a rice pudding or barley porridge
6 *ozs. sugar*   1 *tablespoon cinnamon*

Put a thin layer of pudding in a fireproof dish and sprinkle it with sugar and cinnamon. Brown it under the grill; then arrange another layer of pudding, sugar and cinnamon. Brown again, and continue in this way until all the pudding, sugar and cinnamon are used. The thinner the layers, the better. Serve hot with milk and jam.

Prune Porridge

6 *ozs. prunes*   *the juice of half a lemon*
2 *ozs. sugar*   2 *ozs. semolina*

Wash the prunes, and let them soak overnight in two pints of water. Cook them with sugar until half done, stir in the semolina gradually and simmer for half an hour. Add the lemon juice and pour onto a dish to cool. Serve cold with milk and sugar.

This may be made with rice instead of semolina, and flavoured with vanilla or cinnamon.

LEFTOVERS: Serve with whipped cream and biscuits.

Rice and Apple Porridge

1 *lb. fresh or* ½ *lb. dried apples*   3 *ozs. rice*   4 *cloves*
rind of a lemon, peeled thinly   1½ *pints water*   2 *ozs. sugar*

Bring the rice to the boil in cold water. When it is half cooked add the apples peeled, cored and cut in pieces, and the sugar, lemon rind and cloves. Simmer in a double saucepan until the apples and rice are done. Turn out to cool, and serve cold with sugar.

LEFTOVERS: Bake, decorated with meringue, in layers with strawberry jam.

Semolina Porridge

Make in the same way as barley porridge (page 66).

Whipped Porridge

2 *lbs. fresh fruit or a large tin*   8 *ozs. semolina*
4 *ozs. sugar*   1 *tablespoon cornflour*

Prepare the fruit in the same way as for berry porridge (page 66) Beat in the semolina and sugar. Simmer half an hour, and add the cornflour made into a paste with cold water. Let it boil a few minutes. Remove it from the fire, and beat with a wooden spoon for about ten minutes or in the electric blender for one minute. When it is whipped quite creamy and light, eat it with milk and sugar.

LEFTOVERS: Serve with stewed fruit.

Dumplings

Meringue Dumplings

3 *whites of egg*   2 *ozs. icing sugar*   *vanilla*

Beat the whites of egg to a stiff froth, add the sieved sugar and a few drops of vanilla essence and beat until smooth and shining. Cook the dumplings by dropping spoonfuls onto boiling soup and letting it simmer until they are firm.

Raisin Dumplings

2 *ozs. sugar*   6 *ozs. flour*
a pinch of salt   6 *ozs. raisins*

Mix the dry ingredients and stir in, gradually, about half a pint of water. Let the dough stand for two hours. Cook large dumplings in boiling water for about five minutes. Serve with fruit and berry soups.

LEFTOVERS: Warm up in lemon sauce and use as a pudding.

Rice Dumplings

4 *ozs. rice*   2 *eggs*   *grated rind of half a lemon*
1 *pint milk*   2 *ozs. butter*   *salt*

Simmer the milk and rice together until the rice is quite soft. Add eggs, butter, grated lemon rind and salt. Drop with a spoon in small balls into boiling milk and simmer for a few minutes. Serve with fruit soups.

LEFTOVERS: Use cold with berry sauce as a sweet.

Almond Dumplings

½ *pint milk*   4 *ozs. raisins*   2 *ozs. sugar*
2 *ozs. semolina*   2 *ozs. chopped almonds*

Cook the semolina in milk and allow it to cool. Add the raisins, almonds and sugar. Drop the mixture in spoonfuls into a fruit soup and simmer for a few minutes. Serve immediately.

LEFTOVERS: Eat cold with jam.

Sauces

In Finland, sauces are used to achieve unusual combinations, such as fried veal and currant sauce, carrot balls with sardine sauce, or spinach cakes and apple sauce. If you enjoy such contrasts, it is rewarding to experiment with new combinations.

Hot Egg Sauce

1 *hard-boiled egg*   4 *ozs. butter*
1½ *teaspoons chopped chives or parsley*

Melt the butter and add the chopped eggs while it is still warm. Sprinkle with chives or parsley, and serve with boiled or steamed fish.

LEFTOVERS: Use in making kedgeree or fish toast.

Cold Egg Sauce

2 *hard-boiled eggs*	4 *tablespoons oil*	1 *teaspoon chives*
salt and pepper	2 *tablespoons vinegar*	1 *teaspoon sugar*

Put the yolks of egg through a sieve and mix them with salt, pepper, sugar and one tablespoonful of oil, added in drops. Mix all this until it thickens, gradually stirring in the rest of the oil. Then add, very gradually, vinegar, chopped chives and chopped whites of egg. Serve cold with fish or salad.

LEFTOVERS: Thin slightly and use as a dressing for cold vegetable salads.

Egg Butter

4 *ozs. butter*   4 *hard-boiled yolks of egg*

Mash the yolks of egg. Whip the butter to a cream, add the yolks of egg and beat until creamy. Serve with new potatoes, hot pasties, etc. (The whites of egg finely chopped make a good decoration for salads).

LEFTOVERS: Pound with fillets of raw herring, finely sliced onion, and pepper and salt, and eat spread on brown bread and butter.

Butter Sauce

4 ozs. butter

Warm the butter a little, and then beat it with a wooden spoon until it is white and creamy. Serve with vegetables, on a separate dish.

Cream Sauce

½ pint cream   salt   ½ tablespoon chopped chives

Beat the cream slightly and season it with chopped chives. Serve with potatoes and cold fish.

LEFTOVERS: Stir into any savoury white sauce.

Sour Sauce

½ pint meat stock   1 teaspoon arrowroot   a pinch of sugar
4 ozs. cream   1 teaspoon made mustard pepper
1 yolk of egg   1 gherkin

Beat the stock, cream and the arrowroot mixed to a paste with cold water over the fire until they boil. Stir in the seasoning and beaten yolks of egg, and continue stirring until cool. Add the gherkin cut in small dice. Serve with fish or meat.

LEFTOVERS: Mix with chopped hard-boiled eggs and eat with bread and butter, or make into sandwiches.

Sour-Sweet Sauce

2 ozs. butter   6 ozs. meat stock   vinegar
2 ozs. breadcrumbs   half a lemon   1 teaspoon sugar
1½ tablespoons flour   ¼ pint cream or evaporated milk

Cook together the flour and half the butter. Add the cream gradually and allow it to boil ten minutes. Brown the breadcrumbs in butter, pour in the stock and bring to the boil. Add the cream, flour, and butter mixture, and boil again. Season with vinegar, lemon juice, grated lemon rind and sugar. Serve with fish and vegetable dishes.

LEFTOVERS: Use cold as a dressing for salads.

Pork Sauce

This sauce is a great favourite in Finland.

4 ozs. fresh pork	1 tablespoon flour	salt and pepper
1 onion	½ pint milk or water	

Cut the pork in slices about quarter of an inch thick, and then into pieces about an inch square, and brown these in a frying pan with slices of onion. Lift out the pork and onions, and keep them hot. Stir the flour into the hot fat, brown it slightly and add the boiling milk or water gradually. Season, and allow it to boil a few minutes, then pour over the pork and onions. This makes a very delicious lunch or supper dish, with plain boiled potatoes.

LEFTOVERS: Serve with stewed rabbit, or use it to warm up pieces of cold chicken.

Sardine Sauce

4 ozs. butter	3 tablespoons flour	lemon juice
3 sardines	¾ pint meat stock	

Skin and bone the sardines and pound them with the butter. Mix in the flour, add gradually the boiling meat stock and boil for ten minutes, stirring all the time. Sharpen with lemon juice. Serve with cold chicken, salad, or egg dishes.

LEFTOVERS: Use for stuffing hard-boiled eggs or for flavouring egg toast.

Carrot Sauce

2 big carrots	¾ pint meat stock	1 tablespoon flour salt
2 ozs. butter	3 tablespoons berry juice or the juice of half a lemon	

Clean the carrots, cut them in pieces and boil them in stock with half the butter. When the carrots are ready, cook the flour with the rest of the butter, and add the carrots and stock gradually. Strain through a sieve, season with juice and salt and bring to the boil. Serve with meat, vegetable, or egg dishes.

LEFTOVERS: Serve piled on grilled steaks of salmon, or eat cold with sardines.

Currant Sauce

1½ tablespoons butter	4 ozs. currants
1½ tablespoons flour	salt, sugar and lemon juice

Wash and boil the currants in half a pint of water. Bring the butter and flour to the boil, stir in the currants with their stock, and boil for ten minutes. Season with salt, sugar and enough lemon juice to give a decided flavour. Serve with fish puddings etc.

LEFTOVERS: Pour over grilled bacon or sausages.

Pickled Cucumber Sauce

3 *small pickled cucumbers*   2 *ozs. butter*
½ *pint meat stock*   2 *tablespoons flour*

Soak the salted cucumbers in water for several hours. Peel and dice them and boil in the stock for a short time. Lift them out. Brown the butter and flour. Stir in the stock and let it boil ten minutes, then add the gherkins. Serve with meat or egg dishes.

LEFTOVERS: Use to moisten and flavour rissoles or minced meat.

Horse-radish Sauce

¼ *pint cream or evaporated milk*   1 *tablespoon flour*
4 *ozs. grated horse-radish*   10 *almonds*   1 *teaspoon sugar*

Mix the flour with cream and boil until it thickens, stirring all the time. Add the chopped almonds, sugar, and horse-radish and bring it to the boil. Serve with meat or with steamed or boiled fish.

LEFTOVERS: Use cold with beef and herring salad, or serve with cold roast beef.

Onion Sauce

½ *pint meat stock*   2 *ozs. butter*   4 *ozs. breadcrumbs*
2 *onions*   2 *tablespoons flour*
4 *ozs. sour berry juice or the juice of a small lemon*

Peel the onions, cut them in slices and cook them half an hour in the stock. Brown the butter and flour, and stir in gradually the onions and stock. Simmer for half an hour, and add the breadcrumbs and berry juice. Bring to the boil and strain. Serve with vegetable, egg and fish dishes.

LEFTOVERS: Pour over eggs *en cocotte*.

73

Spinach Sauce

6 *yolks of egg*   2 *ozs. butter*   *lemon juice*
1 *tablespoon flour*   *mushroom ketchup* 4 *ozs. fresh spinach*
salt and vinegar

Beat the butter, flour, lemon juice, two yolks of egg and a little mushroom ketchup over the fire until they thicken. Wash the spinach, put it in a saucepan with the water which clings to the leaves, and bring it to the boil. When it is cooked drain it, put it through a sieve, and mix it with the sauce. Bring the sauce to the boil and season it with salt and vinegar. Serve with fish or egg dishes.

LEFTOVERS: Thicken the sauce with flour and use for filling omelets.

Sweet Sauces

Whipped Cream Sauce

½ *pint cream*   1 *tablespoon icing sugar*
cochineal or any other colouring

Whip the cream until stiff and add the sieved sugar. Colour according to your pleasure, and serve with sweets or stewed fruit.

Berry Juice Sauce

½ *pint berry juice (raspberry, loganberry, red currant etc.)*
juice of half a lemon   1 *teaspoon arrowroot*   *sugar*

Sweeten the berry juice and stir in the arrowroot made into a smooth paste with water. Stir over the fire until it boils, then allow it to cool. Serve cold.

Almond Sauce

1 *gill cream*   1 *oz. sugar*
2 *ozs. almonds*   1 *or 2 yolks of egg*

Peel the almonds and chop them very finely, Beat together the cream, almonds, sugar and yolks of egg, and then stir them over the fire until the mixture thickens but does not boil. Remove it from the fire, and beat it until it is quite cold.

Prune Sauce

| ½ pint cream | 1 yolk of egg | 1 gill water |
| 2 ozs. prunes | 1 oz. sugar | |

Soak the prunes overnight in the water and then boil them until they are tender. Remove the stones and chop them very finely, adding part of the water in which they have been cooked. Beat the yolks of egg and sugar, and add the prunes and boiling cream, beating hard. Heat the mixture in a double boiler until it thickens, beating all the time. Remove from the fire, and beat until cold.

Bread and Cakes

The traditional oven in a Finnish farm house is made of bricks and is often six feet deep, and nearly a yard wide. It is built into the wall like a tunnel, behind the stove. Before baking, a wood fire is lit in the oven. When the embers are red and glowing, they are raked forward and into the fire in the stove with a long wooden pole shod with iron. The oven is then cleaned with a birch twig besom, dipped in water. There is a ventilator at the back of the stove to draw off the smoke. This is closed as soon as the fire is raked out. There is also a damper which can be opened to reduce the heat if necessary.

In the farm houses the bread is baked at home, and rye bread is generally used, except on special occasions. In the North and South, they bake large oval loaves of soft brown bread about two inches thick, and sometimes a bread made with milk and water and a mixture of rye and wheat flour.

In Karelia, the bread is very hard, and is made in large thin rings. Every three or four months, the farmer's wife and all her women have a baking day. Working from early morning, they bake enough bread to last until next baking. The rings are threaded on long sticks and hung under the beams in the kitchen, where they become gradually harder and drier.

In ordinary houses there are usually two or three kinds of bread, sliced, on the table.

The difficulty of heating country ovens has given rise to this habit of baking great quantities at a time, and probably suggested the little cakes and biscuits which are given here. These will be found very useful, as they can be kept in a tin for many weeks and are always ready for an unexpected guest.

Simple Wheaten Bread

1 *pint milk*	4 *ozs. sugar*	3 *eggs*
2 *lbs. plain flour*	3 *heaping teaspoons dried yeast*	

Beat two of the eggs with the sugar and add the milk, flour and yeast which has been mixed with flour. Knead until the dough does not cling to the hands. Cut it in pieces and form with the hands into long rolls about the thickness of three fingers. Taking three at a time, twist them into plaits about eighteen inches long. Brush them with beaten egg and bake in the oven (400°) for about twenty minutes. Cut in slices about an inch thick and serve with coffee or tea. This bread is eaten quite plain without butter. It is very delicious when it is new. Fancy breads are used almost entirely to replace bread and butter in Finland.

Baking Tin Bread

1 *oz. yeast*	4 *ozs. sugar*	6 *ozs. melted butter*
2 *eggs*	½ *pint luke-warm milk*	1 *lb. flour*

ALMOND MIXTURE

6 *ozs. almonds*	6 *ozs. melted butter*
6 *ozs. brown sugar*	4 *tablespoons flour*

Make the mixture in the same way as wheaten bread and after it has risen put it into a greased baking tin about one inch deep Mix the chopped almonds with the sugar, flour and melted butter. Pour the mixture over the bread and bake in a good oven.

Birthday Ring

In Finland they celebrate both the birthday and the name day, which is the feast of the saint whose name you bear. Instead of a birthday cake they bake a large ring of plaited bread. The ring is usually laid on a wide tray which is covered with a white cloth. Inside the ring small cakes or flowers are laid.

A ring is also baked for weddings or funerals.

1 oz. yeast   6 ozs. sugar   1¼ lbs. flour
2 yolks of egg   ½ pint luke-warm milk   3 or 4 ozs. creamed
4 ozs. ground cardamoms   butter

FOR GARNISHING

1 egg   4 ozs. almonds   2 ozs. granulated sugar

Mix the yeast into a paste with some of the milk and stir in flour until it is thick and creamy, then put it in a warm place to rise. When it has risen and is covered with bubbles, add the beaten yolks of egg, sugar, milk, cardamoms, creamed butter and the rest of the flour. Knead the mixture very well, and then form the dough into rolls about one inch thick. Plait them, and join the ends to form a ring. It is also useful to make spare pieces of plait, and then as slices are cut from the ring they may be replaced. Allow the bread to rise on a baking sheet, and then brush it with beaten egg and sprinkle with sugar and chopped almonds. Bake in a good oven.

Sunday Balls

1 tablespoon yeast   3 eggs   ¼ pint luke-warm milk
14 ozs. flour   4 ozs. sugar   4 ozs. melted butter

FOR DECORATING

1 egg   2 ozs. almonds   1 tablespoon granulated sugar

Prepare the mixture as above, then roll it into small balls and after they have risen brush them with beaten egg, and sprinkle with chopped or halved almonds. Bake in a good oven.

Butter Rusks

1 oz. yeast   ½ teaspoon salt   ½ pint luke-warm milk
1¼ lbs. flour   1 oz. sugar   4 ozs. creamed butter

Mix the yeast into a cream with a little luke-warm water, stir in enough flour to make a paste, and allow it to rise. Mix some of the flour with luke-warm milk, add the risen yeast and the rest of the flour. Then put it in a warm place and when it has risen twice its height, add the salt, sugar and butter. Knead well on a pastry board, and form into rolls about one inch thick. Allow them to rise nearly as high again, and bake in a good oven. When they are cool, cut them in slices about one inch thick. Cut each slice in half, and crisp in a good oven.

Baked Spice Crusts

slices of stale bread   butter   4 ozs. granulated sugar
2 ozs. almonds   1 egg   1 tablespoon ground cinnamon
¼ pint cream or evaporated milk

Butter the slices and dip them in a mixture of egg and cream. Sprinkle the buttered side with chopped almonds, sugar and cinnamon, and crisp them in a moderate oven.

Large Cakes

Sugar Cake

6 tablespoons sugar   3 tablespoons cornflour   4 eggs
vanilla or almond essence   4 tablespoons flour

Beat the yolks of egg and the sugar for about a quarter of an hour. Add the flour, almond essence or vanilla, and lastly fold in the whites of egg, beaten to a stiff froth. Pour the mixture into a greased cake tin which has been sprinkled with breadcrumbs, and bake about one hour.

Carrot Cake

4 eggs   8 ozs. sugar   1 tablespoon cinnamon
8 ozs. almonds   8 ozs. cooked carrot

Beat the yolks of egg and sugar until creamy, add the cinnamon, the almonds chopped with the skin on, the carrots rubbed through a sieve and lastly, the whites of egg beaten to a stiff froth. Bake in the same way as sugar cake.

Mary's Cake

1 egg   6 ozs. sugar   6 ozs. melted butter
1 lemon   5 ozs. flour   5 ozs. cornflour
2 tablespoons brandy or sherry

Melt the butter, allow it to re-set and beat it to a cream. Beat the yolks of egg and sugar until creamy and add the butter, lemon juice, grated rind of lemon, brandy and flour and fold in the beaten whites of egg. Bake as above.

Honey Cake

4 eggs	8 ozs. sugar	½ teaspoon dried orange peel
8 ozs. flour	4 ozs. brown honey	¼ teaspoon ginger

Beat well the yolks of egg and half the sugar. Warm the honey and the rest of the sugar. Beat these until they are cool and add them to the sugar and egg. Stir in the flavouring and flour and lastly, the beaten whites of egg. Pour the mixture into a greased cake tin which has been sprinkled with breadcrumbs and bake about one and a half hours.

Telephone Cake

2 eggs 8 ozs. sugar	½ teaspoon soda	8 ozs. flour
rind of one lemon	½ pint cream	4 ozs. cornflour

Beat the eggs and half the sugar until creamy. Add the rest of the sugar, the soda mixed with the cream, which has been whipped, grated lemon rind and flour. Bake as above for about an hour.

Soft Spice Cake

1 egg	½ teaspoon cinnamon	1 oz. melted butter
4 ozs. sugar	½ teaspoon soda	10 ozs. flour
¼ teaspoon ground cardamom	½ teaspoon ground ginger	
1 teaspoon grated orange peel	¼ pint cream or milk	

Beat the egg and sugar until creamy. Add the flavouring, melted butter, soda mixed with cream, and flour. Bake for an hour.

Brown Sugar Cake

6 eggs	12 ozs. brown sugar	1 teasp. gr. cardamom
½ teasp. gr. cloves	1 teasp. cinnamon	8 ozs. flour

Beat the eggs and sugar for a quarter of an hour. Stir in the flour and seasoning and bake about an hour.

Currant Cake

8 ozs. butter	8 ozs. flour	half a lemon
5 eggs	8 ozs. sugar	4 ozs. currants

Beat the butter to a cream. Add one egg, two tablespoonfuls of flour and two tablespoonfuls of sugar and beat well. Continue until all the eggs are used, and then stir in the rest of the flour and sugar, the currants, lemon juice and grated rind of lemon. Bake in a good oven for about an hour.

Rex Cake

1 *lb. rectangular sweet biscuits*
8 *ozs. butter*   8 *ozs. sugar*   3 *eggs*
4 *tablespoons strong black coffee, or coffee essence to taste*

Melt the butter and allow it to re-set. Beat the yolks of egg and sugar until creamy and add the butter, coffee, and whites of egg lightly beaten. Choose an oblong tin or dish of a size to hold a layer of the biscuits, line it with greaseproof paper. (In Finland this cake is made with a special biscuit, and tins of exactly the right size are sold). Spread the inside of the tin with the cream mixture. Arrange the biscuits in layers with coffee filling between, covering the whole cake with the mixture. Stand it in a warm place for a short time to allow the cream to penetrate the biscuits. Put it in a cool place to set, and turn it out next day. It will keep for a long time.

Biscuit Cake

1 *lb. crisp oblong sweet biscuits*
1 *portion of vanilla cream made in the same way as the coffee cream used for Rex cake above.*

Lay the biscuits side by side in a long row on a dish, and pour a layer of vanilla cream over them. Repeat this in layers until all the biscuits are used. Cover all over with the vanilla cream and put in a cool place to set. Cut in slices and serve.

Small Cakes

Cream Cakes

½ *pint cream or evaporated milk*   4 *eggs*   10 *ozs. flour*
2 *tablespoons sugar*   1 *tablespoon chopped almonds*
grated rind of one lemon   *chocolate icing*

Beat the cream well and whip the whites of eggs to a stiff froth. Beat the yolks of egg and sugar, and stir in the cream, flavouring, flour and whites of egg. Put the mixture into small greased cake tins and bake for about quarter of an hour in a good oven. When they are cool cover the cakes with chocolate icing.

Foam Cakes

4 ozs. butter   8 ozs. flour   5 eggs
lard or vegetable shortening for frying

Bring the butter to the boil with half-a-pint of water, add the flour and boil until the mixture no longer sticks to the saucepan. Bear the mixture until it is cool, and whip in the eggs. Drop it in small spoonfuls into smoking hot lard, and fry golden brown. Drain the cakes thoroughly on soft white paper.

Sand Cakes

8 ozs. flour   3 ozs. sugar   ¼ teaspoon salt
6 ozs. butter   1 egg

Mix the egg, salt and sugar with the flour, and then stir in the butter, slightly melted. Allow it to stand two hours. Put the mixture into small cake tins in a layer about a quarter of an inch thick round the sides, and over the bottom, leaving a hollow in the middle. Bake in a good oven.

Nut Cakes

1 portion of sand cake mixture
3 ozs. shelled walnuts   2 tablespoons water   1 oz. butter
grated rind of one lemon   2 ozs. sugar   1 oz. flour

Put the sand cake mixture in small tins, leaving a hollow in the middle, and bake until half done. Shell the nuts and pound them finely in a mortar. Add the sugar, lemon rind, butter and flour. Fill the sand cakes with this mixture and brown them lightly.

Runeberg Tarts

1 portion of sand cake mixture   glacé icing
a little raspberry jam

Put the sand cake mixture into a large tin in a layer about two inches deep. Cut it into round cakes, using the top of a glass, and lift them out onto a greased baking sheet. Bake them a light brown. When they are cool cover them with glacé icing, and put a little jam on each.

Small Cakes and Biscuits for Keeping

These cakes are very useful as they can be made in large quantities and kept in a tin to be enjoyed at any moment.

Ginger Cakes

8 *ozs. sugar*	8 *ozs. butter*	1 *teaspoon soda*
8 *ozs. syrup*	1 *small egg*	1 *lb. flour*
½ *teaspoon ground cardamom*		½ *teaspoon powdered cloves*
half a glass of cream or		½ *teaspoon ginger*
evaporated milk		

Mix the sugar, syrup and seasoning and bring them to the boil. Cool them and stir in the soda mixed with cream, and the beaten egg. Cream the butter and beat it in, and lastly the flour. Stand the mixture in a cool place overnight. The next day take the mixture in convenient portions and roll it out about one eighth of an inch thick on a floured board, using as little flour as possible. Cut it into stars, hearts or crescents, or any other shape. Lay these on a greased baking sheet, fairly far apart, and bake them in a good oven until nice and brown.

Deacon's Ginger Cakes

1 *egg*	4 *ozs. syrup*	1 *teaspoon soda*
8 *ozs. sugar*	2 *ozs. almonds*	¾ *lb. flour*
4 *ozs. melted butter*		1 *teaspoon powdered cinnamon*
1 *teaspoon ground cardamom*		1 *teaspoon ground ginger*
¼ *pint cream or evaporated milk*		

Beat the eggs and sugar until creamy, add the syrup, melted butter, cream mixed with soda, chopped almonds, flavouring and flour. Beat well, roll the mixture out until it is about a quarter of an inch thick, and bake in the same way as ginger cakes.

Soft Ginger Cakes

6 ozs. syrup	4 ozs. butter	1 teaspoon soda
2 ozs. sugar	3 eggs	12 ozs. flour

½ teaspoon ground cloves   ½ teaspoon ground cardamom
½ teaspoon cinnamon   ½ teaspoon ground ginger
1 tablespoon dried orange   ½ tablespoon cream or evaporated
    peel, minced or pounded   milk

Bring the syrup to the boil, remove it from the fire and stir in the sugar. Add the flavouring, creamed butter, soda mixed with cream, beaten eggs and flour and stand overnight. Using a floured board, but as little flour as possible, form the dough into long rolls about one and a half inches thick, and cut each roll into pieces about one and a half inches long. Take each piece and roll it very lightly into a ball using the palms of the hands. These balls may be made bigger or smaller as preferred. Bake in a good oven.

Ginger Spice Cakes

¼ pint cream or evaporated milk   6 ozs. syrup
8 ozs. sugar   1 teaspoon soda   12 ozs. flour
1 teaspoon cinnamon   1½ tablespoons ground ginger
1 teaspoon powdered cloves   2 tablespoons dried orange peel

Beat the cream and add the other ingredients. Mix well and roll out thinly. Cut into small rounds with a pastry cutter and brush them over with warm water. Bake in a good oven.

Ginger Slices

3 eggs   2 ozs. almonds   8 ozs. brown sugar
4 ozs. butter   ½ teaspoon soda   ½ teaspoon ground cardamom
½ teaspoon cinnamon   ½ teaspoon ginger   12 ozs. flour

Beat the eggs and sugar together. Chop the almonds with the skin on and add them to the creamed butter, eggs, sugar and seasoning. Stir in the soda mixed with a little of the flour, and the rest of the flour. Stand overnight. Form with the fingers into long rolls about an inch thick, and bake these in a good oven. While they are still warm, cut them into diagonal slices about an inch thick and crisp them in a cool oven.

Currant Ginger Slices

3 eggs   ½ teaspoon cinnamon   ½ teaspoon soda
8 ozs. sugar   2 ozs. currants   12 ozs. flour
2 ozs. melted butter   2 ozs. cream or evaporated milk

Prepare and bake in the same way as ginger slices.

Cinnamon Nuts

2 eggs   8 ozs. brown sugar   1 teaspoon cardamom
12 ozs. flour   ½ teaspoon cinnamon   4 ozs. melted butter
½ tablespoon chopped orange peel taken from marmalade
¼ pint cream or evaporated milk   1 small teaspoon soda

Beat the eggs and sugar with the flour, creamed butter, soda mixed with cream, and the flavouring. Prepare and bake in the same way as soft ginger cakes.

White Cinnamon Nuts

2 eggs   ½ teaspoon soda   1 teaspoon cinnamon
4 ozs. sugar   1 lb. flour   1 teaspoon cardamom
1 teaspoon ground ginger   2 tablespoons melted butter
6 tablespoons cream or evaporated milk

Make in the same way as cinnamon nuts, but roll each ball in granulated sugar before baking.

Brown Sugar Cakes

3 eggs   the peel of half an orange
6 ozs. brown sugar   ½ teaspoon soda   10 ozs. flour

Beat the eggs and sugar, add the chopped orange peel, and the soda mixed with the flour. Using two spoons, form the dough into small balls, and lay these on a greased baking sheet. Bake in a good oven.

Small Tea Balls

4 yolks of egg   vanilla   4 tablespoons melted butter
8 ozs. sugar   8 ozs. flour   8 ozs. cornflour
4 tablespoons cream or evaporated milk   ½ teaspoon soda

Beat the yolks of egg and sugar. Stir in the vanilla, melted butter, soda mixed with cream, and the flour. Roll into small balls in the same way as soft ginger cakes and bake in a good oven.

Raspberry Balls

1 egg   4 ozs. butter   12 ozs. flour
4 ozs. sugar   4 ozs. sour cream   raspberry jam
1 teaspoon baking powder

Beat the eggs and sugar. Add the creamed butter, the flour mixed with baking powder and the cream. Roll the mixture into small balls, press a hollow with the thumb in the middle of each, and fill it with raspberry jam. Bake in a moderate oven till brown.

Almond Balls

3 eggs   4 ozs. almonds
8 ozs. sugar   8 ozs. flour

Beat the eggs and sugar very well, and add the chopped almonds and flour. Allow the mixture to stand for a few hours. Make small balls, rolling them in granulated sugar, and bake in a good oven.

Principal's Cakes

4 ozs. melted butter   1 yolk of egg   6 ozs. flour
6 ozs. sugar   6 ozs. almonds
FOR BRUSHING
2 whites of egg   3 tablespoons chopped pistachio nuts

Melt the butter and allow it to re-set. Add the sugar and beat to a cream. Stir in the yolks of egg gradually and the chopped almonds and flour. Roll out the mixture and cut it into triangles. Brush these with beaten white of egg, sprinkle with pistachio nuts and brown lightly in a good oven.

Master and Mistress Cakes

8 ozs. butter   4 ozs. cornflour   raspberry jam
3 ozs. sugar   8 ozs. flour

Beat the butter and sugar to a cream and add the flour. Roll out the mixture and cut it into small round cakes, using the top of a glass. Cover half of each round with raspberry jam, then fold them over and pinch the edges together. Bake in a good oven.

Soda Cakes

1 lb. flour   1 teaspoon cinnamon   ¼ pint milk or cream
8 ozs. sugar   1 teaspoon soda   3 ozs. melted butter

Mix the butter and the dry ingredients with a wooden spoon and add the milk gradually. Roll the mixture out and prick it all over with a fork. Cut it into small round cakes. Bake in a good oven.

Marstrand's Biscuits

4 ozs. butter   ¼ pint cream or evaporated milk   8 ozs. flour
4 ozs. sugar   ½ teaspoon soda   8 ozs. cornflour

Beat the sugar and butter till creamy and add the beaten cream. Add alternately cornflour, and flour mixed with soda. Roll the mixture out, prick it and cut it into small round biscuits. Cut a small hole in the centre of each, using a thimble. Bake in a moderate oven.

Rolled Oat Biscuits

10 *ozs. rolled oats*	5 *ozs. butter*	½ *teaspoon soda*
10 *ozs. lard*	10 *ozs. sugar*	10 *ozs. milk* 1 *lb. flour*

Mix the oats, butter and lard thoroughly. Add gradually the sugar, soda mixed with milk, and flour. Let the mixture stand overnight. Roll it out thinly, prick, and cut it into small rounds. Bake in a moderate oven.

Rolled Oat Cakes

2 *eggs*	4 *ozs. butter*	5 *bitter almonds*
8 *ozs. sugar*	1 *lb. rolled oats*	2 *ozs. flour*

Beat the sugar and the eggs. Add the melted butter, oats, chopped almonds and flour. Using two spoons form into small balls, and brown them lightly on a baking sheet in a good oven.

Aniseed Cakes

1 *egg*	5 *ozs. sugar*	1 *teaspoon chopped aniseed*
4 *yolks of egg*	4 *ozs. butter*	10 *ozs. flour*

FOR BRUSHING
One white of egg and chopped aniseed.

Beat the eggs and sugar and add the beaten butter, aniseed and flour. Roll the mixture out and cut it into pieces about two inches long and half an inch wide. Brush these with white of egg, sprinkle with chopped aniseed, and brown in a quick oven.

Butter Stars

8 *ozs. butter*	1 *oz. bitter almonds*
8 *ozs. sugar*	14 *ozs. flour*

FOR BRUSHING
1 *white of egg, granulated sugar, and chopped almonds*

Mix the butter, chopped almonds, sugar and flour together. Roll out the mixture and make small stars, using a cutter. Brush these with white of egg, sprinkle with sugar and chopped almonds, and bake in a good oven.

Butter Rings

8 *ozs. butter*	4 *ozs. sugar*	1 *lb. flour*
2 *tablespoons brandy or sherry*		

Mix all the dry ingredients and add the butter and brandy. Mix well and, using a forcing bag or syringe, press into ribbed strips and twist them into rings. (The rings can also be made from rolls of paste and shaped by hand). Bake in a good oven.

Vanilla Rings

6 ozs. butter	1 egg	vanilla
4 ozs. sugar	3 ozs. almonds	8 ozs. flour

Beat the sugar and butter to a cream and add the beaten egg, chopped almonds, vanilla and flour. Make into small rings as above, and bake in a good oven.

Crisp Fingers

8 ozs. butter	6 bitter almonds
2 tablespoons sugar	12 ozs. flour

FOR BRUSHING
one white of egg and chopped almonds

Cream the butter and sugar and beat in the other ingredients. Mix well and make long rolls about the thickness of a finger. Cut these into strips about two and a half inches long. Brush them with beaten white of egg, roll them in chopped almonds and bake in a good oven.

Cinnamon Fingers

3 eggs	10 ozs. butter	14 ozs. flour
8 ozs. sugar	3 teaspoons cinnamon	

FOR COATING
granulated sugar and almonds

Beat the eggs and sugar and add the creamed butter, cinnamon and flour. Shape and bake in the same way as crisp fingers (page 87), rolling them in granulated sugar and chopped almonds.

Tea Cigars

3 eggs	8 ozs. brown sugar	½ teaspoon cinnamon
12 ozs. flour	1 oz. chopped almonds	candied peel
2½ tablespoons melted butter	½ teaspoon soda	

Beat the eggs and sugar and add the melted butter, cinnamon, chopped almonds, soda and flour. Roll the mixture into fingers the shape of cigars. Decorate each cigar with a slice of candied peel, and bake in a moderate oven.

Antler Cakes

1 egg	4 ozs. sugar	½ teaspoon chopped cardamom
2 ozs. butter	1 teaspoon soda	2 yolks of egg
8 ozs. flour	4 ozs. cornflour	2 ozs. cream or evaporated milk

Beat the eggs and sugar, add the creamed butter, cardamoms, cream, soda, salt and flour. Roll the mixture out about a quarter of an inch thick and then cut it into pieces about two inches long

G

and one inch wide. About three quarters of an inch from each end of every piece make a crosswise cut, about half the width of the slice. Take the ends of the slices and draw them round to form a curve, so that the cuts open a little. Bake in a moderate oven.

Sugar " S " Cakes

3 eggs   6 ozs. sugar   4 ozs. butter   12 ozs. flour

Beat the eggs and sugar, and stir in the creamed butter and flour. Using the fingers, make long thin rolls about the thickness of a pencil, and cut them into strips about two and a half inches long. Roll each piece in sugar and cinnamon, and form into " S " shapes on a greased baking tin. Bake in a moderate oven.

Almond " S " Cakes

3 eggs   8 tablespoons melted butter   12 ozs. flour
8 ozs. sugar   4 ozs. almonds

Beat the eggs and sugar and add the butter, which has been melted and allowed to re-set, and then beaten to a cream. Stir in the chopped almonds and flour. Make into " S's " as above, first rolling the shapes in sugar and chopped almonds.

Special " S " Cakes

4 ozs. butter   3 eggs   ½ teaspoon soda
12 ozs. sugar   1 teaspoon cinnamon   1 lb. flour

Beat the butter and sugar till creamy. Add the beaten eggs, soda, cinnamon and flour. Make in the same way as sugar " S " cakes, rolling them in cinnamon and castor sugar.

Egg Rings

3 eggs   8 ozs. sugar   ½ teaspoon soda
½ pint cream or evaporated milk   1 lb. flour

Beat the eggs and sugar, add the soda mixed with cream, and the flour. Mix well and with the fingers make long rolls about the thickness of a pencil. Cut them into pieces about three inches long and twist them into rings. Brown lightly in a good oven.

Water Rings

3 eggs   4 ozs. sugar   8 ozs. flour
½ teaspoon powdered cardamoms

Beat the eggs and sugar and add the cardamoms and flour. Let the mixture stand a few hours, and make into rings as above. Dip them into boiling water, and bake in a good oven.

Corkscrews

3 eggs   their weight in sugar   a little less flour than sugar

Mix the eggs and sugar, stir in the flour, and pour the mixture with a spoon onto a greased baking sheet in strips about six inches long. Bake these in a moderate oven and as soon as they are cooked twist them into corkscrews and allow them to cool.

Sugar Cakes

3 eggs   their weight in castor sugar and in flour.

Beat the eggs and sugar for a quarter of an hour and add the flour. Drop small spoonfuls onto a baking sheet covered with greaseproof paper. Sprinkle them with sugar and bake in a good oven. Lift the cakes from the paper with a knife.

Almond Cakes

2 whites of egg   6 ozs. almonds
6 ozs. castor sugar   1 teaspoon cinnamon

Beat the sugar and whites of eggs for a quarter of an hour. Clean the almonds with a dry towel, chop them with the skins on and add them with the cinnamon to the mixture. Roll the mixture out thinly, cut into rounds and bake in a moderate oven.

Vanishing Cakes

3 whites of egg   grated rind of one lemon   a few almonds
½ lb. castor sugar   6 ozs. flour   the juice of one lemon

Beat the whites of egg and add gradually the sugar, the lemon rind, lemon juice and the flour. Form into small cakes with two spoons and decorate with sliced almonds. Bake in a cool oven on a greased baking sheet.

Coconut Cakes

4 whites of egg   8 tablespoons castor sugar   4 to 6 ozs. coconut

Whip the whites of egg to a stiff froth and beat them for a quarter of an hour. Add the sugar and coconut very gradually. Drop with a spoon in small high mounds onto a baking sheet which has been greased and sprinkled with cornflour. Stand in a very cool oven until they are set.

Parvula's Nuts

3 eggs   8 ozs. flour   lemon essence or lemon juice
8 ozs. brown sugar   ½ teaspoon soda   2 ozs. chopped almonds

Beat the eggs and sugar, add the chopped almonds, flour mixed with soda, and enough lemon to make a pleasant flavour. Make the mixture into small balls in the same way as soft ginger cakes and bake them in a good oven.

Chocolate Cakes

3 whites of egg   8 ozs. icing sugar   4 ozs. grated chocolate

Beat the whites of egg and add gradually the icing sugar and grated chocolate. Drop with a spoon in small mounds onto a greased baking sheet and bake in a good oven.

Chestnut Fingers

6 ozs. butter   4 ozs. sugar   vanilla essence to taste
2 eggs   6 ozs. flour   8 ozs. peeled cooked chestnuts

Beat the butter well and add one egg, and the sugar, vanilla, flour, and the chestnuts, chopped. Roll into small fingers and brush them with beaten egg. Sprinkle them with sugar and brown lightly in a moderate oven.

Chocolate Fingers

4 ozs. butter   4 ozs. chocolate   4 ozs. flour
4 ozs. sugar   4 eggs

Beat the butter and sugar until creamy and add the melted chocolate, yolks of egg, flour, and lastly the beaten whites of egg. Pour the mixture onto a baking sheet and cook in a low oven. While it is still hot, cut strips about three inches long and one inch broad to make fingers.

Coffee Cakes

4 ozs. black coffee, or as much coffee essence as you like
1 lb. sugar   4 whites of egg

Mix half the sugar with the coffee. Cook until it is quite thick and then let it cool. Beat the whites of egg to a stiff froth, add the remaining sugar gradually, and then the coffee and sugar mixture. Drop spoonfuls onto a greased baking sheet and cook for ten minutes in a good oven. As soon as they are done, press the cakes together in pairs.

Drinks

Kalevala, the Finnish national epic, which was handed down verbally for generations, gives a wonderful picture of the life of the Finns in the distant past. Woven into tales of heroes and witches are charming pictures of country life, much as it is to-day.

Home-brewed ale was popular and in the xxth Rune there is a description of how ale was first made by Osmotar who, hearing the hops crying to the barley and the water in the well that life in solitude was weary,

> " Took on this, the grains of barley,
> Gathered six of grains of barley,
> Seven hop-tassels next she gathered,
> And eight ladles took of water,
> Then upon the fire she placed it,
> And allowed it there to simmer,
> And she boiled the ale of barley
> Through the fleeting days of summer."

But the ale would not ferment, so Osmotar told the squirrel to climb a tall pine tree.

> " From the pine he broke the pine-cones,
> From the fir the leafy tassels,
> In his claws he hid the pine-cones,
> And within his paws he rolled them."

These were put into the ale, but it still refused to ferment, so Osmotar sent the marten,

> " To the Bear's own rocky cavern,
> Where the forest bears are prowling,
> Where the bears are always fighting,
> Where they lurk in all their fierceness.
>
> . . . . .
>
> From the bears' mouths foam was dropping,
> From their furious jaws exuding;
> In his hands the foam he gathered,
> With his paws the foam collected."

Even this failed to produce fermentation, so Osmotar created a bee which flew off to an unmown meadow on an island.

> " Then he soaked his wings with honey,
> Plunged his plumes in liquid honey,
> From the brightest of the herbage,
> From the tips of golden flowerets;
>
> . . . . . .
>
> " And the beer at length fermented,
> And the fresh drink now foamed upwards,
> From within the new-made barrels,
> From within the tubs of birchwood."

But Osmotar was mortified when the ale foamed up to the handles of the tubs and gushed upon the floor, until a throstle sang from the roof:

> " No, the ale is not so worthless;
> 'Tis the best of ale for drinking;
> If into the casks you pour it,
> And should store it in the cellar,
> Store it in the casks of oak wood,
> And within the hoops of copper."

In the XXIIIrd Rune, part of which reads very much like Mrs. Beeton's Household Management, the young bride is instructed in all the domestic arts, including home-brewing.

> " When the malt begins to sweeten,
> Take thou up the malt and taste it.
> With the rake disturb it never,
> Do not use a stick to turn it.
> Go thou often to the malthouse,
> Do not let the sprout be injured,
> Let the cat not sit upon it,
> Or the tom cat sleep upon it."

All this makes the recipes which follow seem very simple.

Home Brewed Ale

3 gallons water   3 ozs. hops   1 oz. yeast
2 lbs. barley malt and ½ lb. rye flour
or 2 lbs. rye malt and ½ lb. barley flour

Heat five pints of water and just before boiling add half a pound of malt, two and a half pints of boiling water and two ounces of flour. Move to the edge of the fire and cover. After an hour, put it on the fire again and just before boiling, add malt and flour. Repeat until all the malt, flour and water are mixed. Leave it for five hours on the side of the stove. Add the hops, heat until nearly boiling and strain. Allow the brew to cool, stir in the yeast mixed with water and put it in a warm place to ferment. If it becomes too frothy, add some pieces of ice. Next day, pour it into a cask and close it. Keep in a cold place. After a few days it is ready to drink.

Simple Home Brew

20 *pints water*   4 *ozs. hops*   1 *tablespoon yeast*
2 *lbs. rye malt*   4 *ozs. sugar*

Heat the water until luke-warm and mix in the malt, hops, sugar and yeast, made into a paste with water. Put it in a warm place and when it begins to ferment, chill it and strain. It can be used at once, or bottled and kept.

Red Currant Ale

10 *pints water*   1 *lb. red currants*   4 *ozs. sugar*
1 *lemon*   2 *ozs. black currant leaves*   2 *ozs. yeast*

Put the water, lemon juice, grated rind of lemon, currants and yeast on the fire and boil for twenty minutes. Strain and add the sugar. When it is luke-warm, add the yeast mixed with water and allow the juice to ferment. When it has fermented sufficiently, chill it by adding a few pieces of ice. Bottle, and keep in a cool place.

Hot Fruit Punch

1 *pint strong cherry juice*   2 *bottles of soda water*
2 *lemons and the juice of* 3 *more lemons*   2 *lbs. sugar*   1 *pint water*

Mix the juice of three lemons with the cherry juice. Heat the sugar with water until you can blow bubbles from a tube dipped into the syrup. Add the cherry juice. Just before serving put the sliced lemons and soda water into a punch bowl and pour over them the boiling syrup. Serve very hot.

Fruit Cup

3 *lemons*   *sugar*   1 *pint cherry or raspberry juice*
1 *pineapple*   5 *bottles of soda water*
20 *blanched almonds*   *small pieces of ice*

Put the berry juice into a large punch bowl and add thin slices of lemon. Peel the pineapple, slice it into small squares and add the almonds, cut in half. Use enough sugar to make the cup rather sweet, then cover the bowl and allow it to stand till the next day. Just before serving, add the soda water and pieces of ice.

Finnish Coffee

Traditional Finnish Coffee is always made in a copper kettle. When the water is boiling hard, a heaping teaspoonful of coffee is added for each cup. It is boiled for ten minutes, and finally a piece of dried fish skin is put into the kettle to clear the coffee. The grounds sink to the bottom, and the coffee is not usually strained, but the last cups must be poured carefully. Cream is usually drunk with coffee instead of milk. In most households, the grounds are boiled up again with water, which is strained off and kept as a basis for the next brew of coffee. The kettle is then scoured with a crescent shaped brush, and burnsihed until it shines.

A coffee party is the equivalent of an English tea party, though there is a growing fashion for five o'clock tea. At a traditional coffee party, the guests sit round the table, which is covered with a large embroidered or patterned cloth. In the centre is a bowl of flowers standing on an embroidered mat and opposite the hostess, the coffee kettle. Sliced sweet bread without butter, rusks, small cakes and biscuits are arranged on dishes. There is generally a large sweet cake which must be sliced before it comes to the table. With the first cup of coffee, sweet bread is eaten. When the first cup is finished the hostess will rise and, walking round the table, re-fill the cups. Small cakes and biscuits accompany the second cup, and slices of cake, often eaten with a spoon, the third. If the party is a long one, the guests will often drink four or five cups of coffee. If there are men present they remain seated while the hostess serves the guests.

Preserving

Fresh fruit and vegetables are hard to get in the long frozen Finnish winter and before the advent of tinned and frozen foods this difficulty had to be overcome by all sorts of preserving. In this country many fresh vegetables are cheap all through the winter, and storage space is often limited, but many of the Finnish ways of keeping vegetables would be useful to people who have gardens with large crops of beans, cabbage, spinach, and so on.

The traditional Finnish method of refrigeration is economical. Country houses are usually built with two cellars beneath them. One of these is kept as an ice chamber. In the spring great blocks of ice about three feet across are cut from the rivers or lakes, and the room is filled from floor to ceiling, leaving just the space of one block by the door. The door has a small opening opposite this ice-bound space which is used as a larder to store milk, cream, butter and other perishable food. The ice lasts all through the summer and the following winter, and is renewed in the spring. The other cellar is kept cool and is used for storing dried and salted vegetables. These would be spoilt by intense cold. If the temperature falls too low, the chill is removed from the air by braziers of charcoal or wood.

Drying

This method is very usual in Finland and nearly all fruit and vegetables may be kept in this way. Sun-drying is difficult, as it takes a long time, and needs constant watching to avoid dust. The most satisfactory way is to spread the fruit or vegetables on trays in a warm place.

95

A very good drier is made from strips of wood joined to form oblong frames. The frames are covered with wire netting, and have a piece of wood about four inches high nailed at each corner as a leg. These frames can be stood one above the other. If the legs of the undermost are put on four bricks, it can be placed over the stove or on the kitchen range. The dampest fruit or vegetables must be put underneath and, as they become drier, be moved higher up.

Dried Apples

Peel and core the apples, cut them in slices and dry them on racks.

Dried Beans

Runner beans can be cut in thin slices and dried.

Dried Cabbage

Tie a string round the cabbage stalk, and hang it upside down. If the outside leaves show any signs of decay, strip them off. Cabbages must not be kept near other vegetables as the damp from the cabbage leaves will make them rot.

Dried Mushrooms

Thread a string through the mushrooms, using a large darning needle, and hang them up in a warm room.

Dried Pears

Peel and core the pears, cut them in half, and dry in a warm place.

Dried Spinach

This is particularly useful as it takes very little space to store and is so concentrated that two tablespoonfuls of dried spinach are equivalent to one and a half pounds of fresh.

Dried Orange Peel

Peel the oranges very finely, and dry the rind in a warm place. This makes a very good and inexpensive flavouring for cakes or puddings.

Salting

All vegetables before salting should be put in hot water and brought to the boil. Drain them carefully and when they are quite cold, put them in a large bowl or tub which has been lined with greaseproof paper. Large vegetables must be cut in pieces before salting. Arrange them in layers with coarse salt and finish with a layer of salt, and cover with several layers of greaseproof paper, or a piece of board. Put a weight of from four to six pounds on top and store the vegetables in a cool place. They must be watched carefully, and any signs of mildew removed. Before using, wash thoroughly, or if they are very salt, soak them overnight.

Salted Beans

Runner beans may be salted in the ordinary way, or kept in a linen bag. Clean and wash the beans, cut off the ends and strip the tough strings from the back. Bring them to the boil in a little salted water. Put them in a linen bag, tie it up, and keep it covered with cold water which has been salted in the proportion of three ounces of salt to each pint of water.

Salted Spinach

Wash the spinach and bring it to the boil, then pour cold water over it. Press it into small hard balls with the hands, and pack them in layers with salt.

Salted Cabbage

Cut small white cabbages into strips and beat them well with a wooden spoon. Put them in layers with small pieces of apple and carrot and sprinkle each layer with salt. (If a wooden tub is used, seal the cracks with a mixture of vinegar and rye flour). Cover with a lid, and put a weight on top so that it is well pressed down. Put it in a warm room for a week to ferment. Remove any mildew, and keep it in a fairly warm place.

Preserving in Water

Various berries and vegetables may be kept for a time in water provided only fresh and sound ones are used. Berries with a tough skin, such as gooseberries and cranberries, are best.

Wash them well, put them in a wooden or glass bowl, and pour enough fresh water over them to cover. Cover with a wooden board and keep in a cool place.

Sour berries are best for preserving in this way. The berries must be either boiled, or mashed raw, and then put into a perfectly clean bowl of wood, china, or glass, and covered over.

Preserves

Carrot Jam

1 *lb. carrots*	1½ *pints water*
3 *lemons*	1 *lb. sugar*

Peel the lemons very finely, cut the rind in thin strips, and cook these in one and a half pints of water until soft. Then lift them out, and parboil the carrots in the same water. Drain, and pour cold water over them. Cook the sugar and lemon juice until it is a thick syrup, then add the carrots and lemon rind, and cook until the carrots are soft and the jam clear. Pour into glass jars and seal.

Use as an accompaniment to cold meat or for cakes and sweets.

Fruit Butter

Whenever a large quantity of fruit is used for jam or jelly making there will be a certain amount of waste, either peel and core of raw fruit, or cooked fruit which has been strained of juice. This can all be made into a preserve which will have many uses.

Rub the fruit through a sieve and simmer it gently with half its weight of sugar for two or three hours. (If you are using raw fruit peelings, simmer these gently with as little water as possible until quite soft, then rub through a sieve). Put into jars in the same way as jam and this fruit butter can be used for flavouring or eaten with cold meat instead of pickles.

Ginger Pears

(Small unripe pears or windfalls may be used)

5 *lbs. small pears*	3 *lbs. sugar*	1 *pint water*
5 *pieces of root ginger*	*juice of one lemon*	

Chop the ginger, and tie it up in a piece of muslin. Put it in water with the sugar and lemon juice, and cook until thick and syrupy. Peel the pears whole, leaving a piece of stalk. Make two crosswise cuts about a quarter of an inch deep on the bottom of each pear, then put them into the syrup and cook until they are soft and clear. Skim well and remove the ginger. Put the pears into glass jars and pour the syrup over them. Seal and keep in a cool place.

Bottled Fruit Juices

Bottled fruit juice is economical to make and easy to store and will be found very useful for flavouring when fresh fruit is scarce.

Apple Juice

10 *lbs. cooking apples*   ½ *lb. sugar to each pint of juice*
6 *pints water*

Wash the apples and cut them in pieces without peeling. Boil in six pints of water until the apples are quite soft. Drain through a muslin without stirring. Cook the juice and sugar for a short time on a hot fire, skimming well, until the juice is quite clear. Pour it while still hot into warmed bottles. Cork at once and keep in a dry, cool, dark place.

Black Currant Juice

7 *lbs. black currants*   3½ *pints water*
¾ *lb. of sugar to each pint of juice*

Wash the berries and crush them, leaving the stalks on. Pour boiling water over them and allow them to ferment for three or four days. Strain through a muslin. Boil the juice on a very hot fire until it is quite clear, and skim carefully. Bottle and keep in the same way as apple juice.

Black and Red Currant Juice

3½ *lbs. cleaned and stalked black currants*
3½ *lbs. cleaned and stalked red currants*
water   1 *lb. sugar to each pint of juice*

Pour enough cold water over the berries to cover them and bring them to the boil. Allow them to simmer until the berries are soft, stirring all the time. Strain through a muslin. Cook with or without sugar on a very hot fire for a short time, skimming well. Pour the hot juice into warmed bottles and cork immediately Keep in a cool dark place.

Cranberry Juice

7 *lbs. cranberries*   1 *pint water*
¼ *lb. sugar to each pint of juice*

Wash the berries and simmer until they are broken. Strain them through a muslin without stirring. Dissolve the sugar in the juice and bring it quickly to the boil, skimming well. Bottle and keep in the same way as apple juice.

Cherry Juice

5 *lbs. cherries*   2½ *lbs. sugar*

Wash the cherries, and put them in alternate layers with sugar in an earthenware casserole. Seal the join between the lid and the casserole with a paste made of flour and water. Stand the casserole in a *bain-marie* and simmer six hours from the time when it comes to the boil. Replenish when necessary with boiling water. Allow the juice to cool, strain it through a muslin and pour it into dry bottles. The pulp of the cherries can be used for sweet soups.

Simple Cherry Juice

5 *lbs. cherries*   ½ *lb. sugar to each pint of cherry juice*

Wash the cherries and crush them with their stones. Allow them to soak overnight. Strain through a muslin and cook the juice with the sugar for a short time on a hot fire. Put the hot juice into warmed bottles.

Gooseberry Juice

7 *lbs. gooseberries*   3½ *pints water*
¾ *lb. sugar to each pint of juice*

Make in the same way as black currant juice.

Berry Juice in a Keg

7 *lbs. black currants*   3½ *lbs. red currants*
7 *lbs. raspberries*   *water*

Wash the currants without removing the stalks and put them with the raspberries into a keg. Pour enough boiling water over them to cover. Put the top lightly onto the keg, and keep from two to four days in an ordinary temperature. Then close the top firmly and keep it in a cool place without moving for six or seven weeks. Strain through a muslin, bottle and cork.

Orange Juice in Citric Acid

Rinds of ten oranges   7 lbs. sugar
5 pints water   2 ozs. citric acid

Grate the orange rinds and mix them with sugar. Pour cold water over the sugar and stir until dissolved. Add the citric acid and when it is thoroughly dissolved, strain the juice, bottle and cork.

Raspberry Juice

7 lbs. raspberries   1 pint water   1 lb. sugar

Put the raspberries into boiling water, cover the pan and keep them hot on the side of the fire for about two hours, not allowing them to boil. Strain through a muslin without disturbing the dregs. Dissolve the sugar in the juice and bring to the boil very quickly. Boil a few minutes and then cool. Bottle and cork carefully.

Fermented Raspberry Juice

7 lbs. raspberries   1 pint water
¾ lb. sugar for each pint of juice

Crush the raspberries in an earthenware bowl. Pour the boiling water over them and allow the berries to ferment about four or five days. If mildew forms, skim it off carefully. Strain through a muslin without disturbing the sediment. Cook in the same way as cranberry juice. Pour into heated bottles, and keep in a cool dark place.

Red Currant Juice

Prepare in the same way as black currant juice.

Red Currant and Raspberry Juice

3½ lbs. of cleaned red currants   3½ lbs. of raspberries
¾ lb. sugar to each pint of juice   water

Mash the raspberries and drain the juice off through a muslin. Pour enough cold water over the currants to cover them and boil until quite soft. Strain through the same muslin as the raspberries, allowing the juices to mingle. Boil the juice with the sugar on a hot fire until clear. Skim well, and bottle.

Rhubarb Juice

7 *lbs. rhubarb cut in pieces*   1 *pint water*

Wash the rhubarb and cook it in water until quite soft. Strain through a muslin without stirring and cook the juice on a hot fire for a short time. Add half a pound of sugar to each pint of juice and pour while still hot into warmed bottles.

Rhubarb and Red Currant Juice

6 *lbs. rhubarb*   6 *pints water*
4 *lbs. red currants*   3 *lbs. sugar*

Wash the rhubarb, cut it in pieces and cook it with the red currants in water until the juice is extracted. Strain through a muslin without stirring. Cook the juice with sugar until it is quite clear, and skim well. Put the hot juice into warmed bottles, and keep in the same way as fermented raspberry juice.

Rhubarb Juice with Lemon

8 *lbs. rhubarb*   *water*
4 *lemons* $\frac{1}{2}$ *lb. sugar to each pint of juice*

Cut the rhubarb in pieces, crush it, and put it into glass jars in layers alternately with sliced lemon. Pour over enough cold water to cover and put a light weight on top. After four days strain the juice. Cook twenty minutes with sugar. Skim well, and then put the hot juice in bottles and keep in a cool, dry, dark place.

Strawberry Juice

2 *ozs. acetic acid*   5 *lbs. strawberries*
2$\frac{1}{2}$ *pints water*   1 *lb. sugar to each pint of juice*

Dissolve the acetic acid in water and pour over the fruit. Let it soak in a cool place for twenty four hours. Strain the juice through a muslin without disturbing the fruit more than necessary Dissolve the sugar in the juice, and bottle.

Whortleberry Juice

7 *lbs. whortleberries*   5 *pints water*

Crush the berries and simmer them in the water until all the juice is extracted. Strain through a muslin. Cook the juice again for a little while and skim well. Pour while still hot into warmed bottles and cork. If the juice is preferred sweet, add a quarter of a pound of sugar to each pint of juice after it has been strained.

Pickles

Sweet pickles or jam are eaten a great deal in Finland with both hot and cold meat; roast lamb with plum pickle, cold beef with pickled melon, or baked ham with gooseberry pickle, are all delightful combinations and there are many others.

Cherry Pickles

3 lbs. cherries	¾ pint water	a stick of cinnamon
¼ pint wine vinegar	1½ lbs. sugar	10 cloves

Wash the cherries and put them into a china bowl. Cook the vinegar, water, sugar and seasoning for a short time. While still hot, pour the liquid over the berries. Cover the bowl and stand for two days. Bring the fruit and juice to the boil. Lift the cherries out and put them into glass jars. Cook the liquid, skimming well until it is thick. Remove the cinnamon, and pour the hot liquid over the berries. Put into glass jars, seal, and keep in a cool place.

Crab Apple Pickle

3 lbs. crab apples	2 pints wine vinegar	1 lb. sugar

Wash the crab apples, prick them and put them into glass jars. Cook the sugar and vinegar and while still hot, pour over the fruit. Next day strain off the juice and cook it for a short time. Skim well and pour hot over the apples. Repeat at intervals of one day until the crab apples are soft, and the juice a little thick. Tie down and keep in a cool place.

Cucumber or Melon Pickle

4 lbs. cucumber or melon	1 lb. sugar	water and salt
1¼ pints wine vinegar	a stick of cinnamon	peppercorns
cloves		

Peel the cucumbers. Cut them in half lengthwise and remove the seeds with a silver spoon. Cut them in big pieces, bring to the boil quickly in a little salted water, and put them on a towel to dry. Tie the spices in a muslin bag and simmer for fifty minutes with the vinegar and sugar. Lift out the spices, pour the hot liquid over the cucumber, cover, and leave it to stand four days. Then strain off the juice, boil it once more and pour it hot over the cucumber. Seal in glass jars, and keep in a cool place. All kinds of melon may be pickled in the same way as cucumber.

Pickled Gherkins

small fresh cucumbers
leaves of black currants, cherry, or oak

horse-radish
mustard seeds

VINEGAR MIXTURE

2 pints vinegar	8 ozs. salt	1 tablespoon acetic acid
10 pints water	3 tablespoons alum	1 tablespoon cloves
1 tablespoon white peppercorns		1 tablespoon blackpeppercorns

Soak the cucumbers overnight in water and wipe them well. Put them into a wooden or earthenware bowl in layers with the various leaves and some pieces of horse-radish spread thickly between so that the cucumbers do not touch each other. Tie the mustard seeds in a muslin bag and put them on top. Tie the other spices in muslin and cook with the vinegar, water, salt, acetic acid and alum. Skim well, strain and pour cold over the cucumbers. Put a light weight on top and cover the bowl with greaseproof paper. Keep in a cool place.

Gooseberry Pickle

2 lbs. green gooseberries		6 ozs. wine vinegar
salt	½ pint water	2 lbs. sugar

Clean the gooseberries, wipe them with a cloth and prick each gooseberry with a skewer. Bring them to the boil quickly in a little salted water, then put them in a towel to dry. When cool, put them in a china bowl. Boil the vinegar, water and sugar until thick and while still hot, pour it over the berries and cover the bowl with a linen cloth, folded many times. After standing for two days strain off the juice, boil it again skimming well, and pour hot over the berries. Repeat twice, at intervals of two days. If the berries are already soft, let the juice cool before pouring it over them. Bottle in the ordinary way and keep in a cool place.

Marrow Pickle

Cut the marrow in half lengthwise and remove the seeds with a silver spoon. Cut the halves in lengthwise strips about an inch thick and soak them overnight in vinegar. The next day cut the strips of marrow in half inch cubes. For every pound of marrow take half a pound of sugar, four ounces of vinegar and three ounces of water. Tie in a bag a piece of cinnamon, a piece of root ginger and half a lemon. Boil in the liquid until thick, lift out the spice bag and add the marrow cubes. Cook until they are clear, but not soft enough to break. Then pour hot into glass jars, seal and keep in a cool place.

Pickled Mushrooms

2 lbs. cleaned button mushrooms   water and salt

VINEGAR MIXTURE

2½ pints vinegar   6 ozs. sugar   ½ tablespoon salt
1 teaspoon grated nutmeg   2 bay leaves   ½ tablespoon cloves
½ tablespoon white peppercorns

Bring the mushrooms to the boil in salted water. Drain them on a towel and when cool put them in glass jars. Tie the seasoning in a muslin bag and boil in the vinegar until it is well flavoured. Lift out the seasoning, and pour the mixture, cold, over the mushrooms. Cover the jars, tie down and keep in a cool place.

Plum Pickle

4 lbs. plums   1½ lbs. sugar   10 cloves
1¼ pints vinegar   a piece of cinnamon

Prick each clove with a needle and put these into a glass jar. Boil the vinegar, sugar and seasoning for ten minutes. Cool the liquid and pour it over the cloves. Cover the jar and stand for a week. Then bring the juice to the boil again with the plums. Lift out the plums and put them into jars. Boil the juice again until it is thick. Skim well, and strain over the plums while still hot. Cover and tie down and keep in a cool place.

Red Currant Pickle

3 lbs. red currants with their juice   ½ pint water   8 cloves
¾ pint wine vinegar   10 ozs. sugar   a piece of cinnamon

Tie sprays of red currants into large bunches. Wash them, spread them on a towel to dry and put them in glass jars. Boil the vinegar, water, sugar and spices until thick. Remove to cool, lift out the cinnamon and pour the liquid over the berries. Cover the jars, tie down and keep in a cool place.

Special Finnish Food

The great Feast Days which mark the rhythms of the year have kept their importance in Finnish national life. In our own country with its uncertain climate the seasons tend to become indistinguishable, but in Finland the sparkling, rigid winter, the majestic break-up of the ice on rivers and lakes and the sudden rush of growth in spring, the glowing summer with its long light nights, and the blue and gold brilliance of autumn have given each season its unmistakable character and each feast its appropriate setting.

The recipes which follow are mostly unsuitable for English everyday life. But they may help to pass a dull moment while the rain drips down the windows.

CHRISTMAS EVE

The tradition of the Christmas turkey is unknown in Finland. Its place is taken by a large baked ham surrounded with prunes and served with potatoes and green peas. The meal begins with various cold foods, temptingly spread out on a sidetable, and then hot fish eaten with potatoes and white sauce, melted butter, and plenty of pepper and salt. Instead of the Christmas pudding there are pastry stars stuffed with prunes.

Christmas Stars

one portion of flaky pastry
FILLING

| 1 *lb prunes* | 2 *pints water* | 6 *ozs. sugar* |

Wash the prunes and soak them for a few hours with water and sugar. Simmer them until tender and then stone and chop them finely. Roll the pastry out until it is a quarter of an inch thick, and then cut it into pieces about two and a half inches square. Make two cuts in from each corner to form the points of the star. Lay a teaspoonful of prune filling in the centre of each tart. Leaving the points of the stars flat on the pastry board, raise the sides and pinch them together so that the prune filling is covered with pastry. Bake quickly in a hot oven and then stand immediately in a cool place. These tarts must first be allowed to cool, but they are usually warmed before eating. During the week before Christmas there are many days of baking when quantities of tarts, ginger cakes and spice biscuits are made, and great plaits of sweet spiced bread.

SHROVE TUESDAY

During Shrove Tuesday, balls stuffed with cream and almonds are eaten with a sweet almond soup.

Shrove Tuesday Balls

| 1 oz. yeast | 4 tablespoons sugar | 1¼ lbs. flour |
| ½ pint luke-warm milk | | 3 ozs. melted butter |

FILLING

| 4 ozs. almonds | 1 tablespoon hot water | ¼ pint cream |
| 4 ozs. sugar | egg for brushing | |

Mix the yeast into a paste with some of the warm milk, and add flour until it is as thick as Devonshire cream. Stand it in a warm place to rise. When the dough has risen and is covered with bubbles, add the sugar, melted butter and the rest of the flour and milk. Cover with a towel, and stand in a warm place until it has risen to twice its height, then turn out onto a floured board and roll into balls about the size of a small apple. Brush them with beaten egg, and bake in a good oven. When the balls are cool, cut a thin slice from each and scoop out some of the inside. Blanch the almonds and dry and chop them. Mix these with the sugar, water, cream and the scooped out crumb. Mix well, and fill the balls, replacing the lid. Eat them with hot milk or almond soup.

Shrove Tuesday Soup

| 3 pints milk | 4 ozs. almonds | 4 ozs. sugar |

Bring the milk to the boil and add the sugar and finely chopped almonds. Boil for ten minutes.

Shrove Tuesday Pancakes

3 eggs	1 lb. buckwheat flour	4 ozs. butter
2 tablespoons yeast	8 ozs. flour	butter for frying
1½ pints milk	a pinch of salt	

Work the melted butter into the flour, cook together and stir in the milk. Boil the mixture for ten minutes, then cool. Stir in the beaten eggs, the yeast mixed to a paste with milk, and the buckwheat flour. Put it in a wam place for several hours to rise and season. Fry pancakes about half an inch thick, browning them on both sides. These are delicious with caviare and melted butter and there are tins and little jars of quite reasonable caviare on the market which are suitable for this purpose. They may also be eaten with cranberry or red currant jelly.

EASTER

The characteristic Easter food is Mammi, which is served in baskets of birch bark, and eaten with cream and sugar.

Mammi

This is usually made in a large iron pot.

| 6 pints water | 2 lbs. rye flour | dried orange peel |
| 1¼ lbs. rye malt | ¼ teaspoon salt | |

Mix five ounces of malt with two pints of water, so nearly boiling that the bubbles are rising, and spread a layer of rye flour over it. Then cover the pot and stand it in a warm place for two hours. Mix well, add two pints of bubbling hot water mixed with another five ounces of malt, and then cover with a layer of rye flour. Stand it in a warm place and mix it at the end of an hour. Repeat at intervals of an hour until all the malt, water and flour are used. Then flavour with salt and finely chopped dried orange peel, and boil for ten minutes, stirring all the time. Stir until the mixture cools, then put it into birch bark boats and bake for three hours in a low oven. It is ready when the edge of the bark is covered with a fine powder. Serve cold with cream and sugar. Mammi is perfectly cooked when the bottom is like a thin layer of syrup.

Easter Loaf

| 1 pint milk | 2 ozs. yeast | 4 ozs. sugar | 3 eggs |
| 2 lbs. flour | 4 ozs. butter | 4 ozs. raisins | |

Mix the milk, yeast and flour, and stand in a warm place to rise. Mix in the creamed butter, raisins and the eggs beaten with the sugar. Shape the dough into a big round loaf. Allow it to rise again and before baking, brush with beaten egg, and sprinkle with sugar, chopped almonds and raisins.

MAY DAY

The first of May is a students' festival. To celebrate the end of the long winter they put on their white caps. When a student wears his cap for the first time the parents will often say, " Now you have your white cap, take care that you keep it clean."

Singing and carrying banners, the students form processions and march through the town and out into the country to their favourite inns. Everyone who has been a student joins them and even old men in faded caps link arms with the rest and sing. Having arrived at an inn, they sit at long tables under the trees and drink Sima and eat dropped cakes.

Sima

| 10 *pints water* | *rinds of two lemons* | 2 *ozs. yeast* |
| 1 *lb. honey* | 2 *ozs. hops* | |

Put the water, sliced lemon rinds and hops on the fire and bring them to the boil. Pour in the honey, cool, and add the yeast mixed with water. Allow the drink to ferment for three or four days, then strain an bottle it. Seal carefully, and keep in a cool place for about a fortnight before using.

Dropped Cakes

| 4 *eggs* | 1 *tablespoon yeast* | 1 *lb. flour* |
| 1 *tablespoon sugar* | 1 *pint luke-warm milk* | *fat for frying* |

Mix the eggs and the sugar, add the yeast stirred into a paste with milk and a little flour, and allow the mixture to rise. Heat the fat until it is just smoking and then drop the mixture into it, two tablespoonfuls at a time, so that it makes pretty swirls. Turn them with a perforated spoon and brown them lightly on both sides Put them on kitchen paper to drain, and sprinkle with sugar.

Sugar Dropped Cakes

| 8 *whites of egg* | 1 *egg* | 6 *ozs. sugar* | 6 *ozs. flour* |

Beat the eggs and sugar and add the flour. Cook in swirls in the same way as dropped cakes.

Midsummer day is a general holiday. In the country there are church services in the morning, and dancing and feasts throughout the day, but the most delightful part of the revels takes place on Midsummer Eve. (Of recent years it has been decided to begin the festival on the Saturday nearest to Midsummer day and some people regret this since even the difference of a few days may spoil the enjoyment of the midnight Sun). At about six o'clock in the evening people have a big dinner beginning with curd soup, followed by boiled salmon and piquant sauce. Afterwards they set out with sandwiches, cakes and a coffee kettle. They go out into the forest, to the top of a hill, or to the shores of a lake, and build great fires of pine and fir branches. Sometimes small tar barrels are piled on the fire and filled with branches until they blaze high and fall. All night long people dance to the music of accordions and brew coffee. In the North of Finland the sun never sets on Midsummer Eve, while in the South, it only dips to make a brief twilight.

Midsummer Curds

10 *pints milk*   1½ *teaspoons rennet*

Put eight pints of milk in a saucepan over a gentle fire and when it reaches blood heat, add the rennet. Allow it to cook for twenty four hours. It may be left for a time to simmer, then taken off, and cooked in stages as convenient, but the total time of cooking must be twenty four hours. After this add the other two pints of milk and bring to the boil. The curds become deep brown and are eaten with sugar.

Karelian Food

In the district of Karelia, the peasants are very hospitable and at weddings or funerals a great feast is held. Preparations are made for days beforehand. The great brick baking ovens are filled with wood fires and then raked clear. After the bread and tarts are baked, earthenware pots of meat are left all night in the gentle warmth.

The first course of the dinner is baked meat, each person having a separate bowl and the importance of the wedding or funeral is gauged by the number of these. Sometimes, there are as many as eighty or a hundred. After this, there are Karelia tarts, with five or six different fillings. Lastly, there is a sweet soup, made with raisins or prunes.

Karelia Baked Meats

1 lb. loin of pork   1 lb. veal
1 lb. mutton   salt, pepper and water

Cut the meat into large pieces, mix together and arrange in alternate layers with salt and peppercorns in an earthenware bowl. Pour in enough water to cover. Bake in a rather slow oven for several hours under a lid. Add more water if necessary. This is sometimes eaten with potatoes.

Karelia Tarts

12 ozs. rye flour   12 ozs. white flour   ¾ pint water   salt
FILLING
2 tablespoons butter   salt
8 ozs. rice   1½ pints milk

Wash the rice and put it into boiling milk with the butter. Simmer until soft. Salt slightly and turn out to cool. To make the pastry, mix the water, salt and flour into a smooth dough and cut into equal sized pieces. Roll into very thin ovals about the size of a hand. Lay the filling in a little pile on each, so that the edges are free. Turn up the sides to form a boat shape and press the edges with the fingers evenly to form little dimples. Bake in a good oven. Cover with a cloth for a short time and while still warm, brush on a mixture of ¼ pint of boiling water and two tablespoonfuls of butter. Eat warm with melted butter or milk. These tarts are usually baked on Saturday night for Sunday. Often they filled with mashed potatoes, carrots or cranberries.

Hame Cheese

5 pints milk   1 teaspoon rennet   salt

Bring the milk over a low fire to blood heat and add the rennet. Allow it to stand in a warm place from ten to fifteen minutes until the curds have formed. When the curds rise, score them across with a knife and let them sink once more. Lift out the cheese from the pan, sprinkle with salt and put it in a shallow dish. Cover with a plate and press well, tipping the dish from time to time to allow the liquid to run away. This cheese is often made in a wooden mould to give it shape. It is eaten with milk or bread and butter. Hame is a district of South Finland.

Norrbottnia Cheese

7 *pints milk*   1 *teaspoon rennet*   *salt*

Warm the milk to blood heat and add the rennet. Let it stand, covered for an hour and a half. Put it on the fire once more and warm it gently until the curd can be lifted out with the hands. Drain off the liquid, pressing the cheese against the bottom of the saucepan, to be sure that it is well drained and then lift out onto a wooden board. Form it into a round about half an inch thick. Bake the cheese in the oven, or in a heavy iron pan over an open fire until it is a nice golden brown. This cheese is most delicious cut in slices and fried in butter, then sprinkled with castor sugar, and eaten with tea or coffee.

Savo Fish Pie

2 *pints water*   4 *ozs. lard*   8 *ozs. fat pork*
2½ *lbs. rye flour*   3 *lbs. fish*   3 *tablespoons salt* *milk*

Mix the flour, melted lard, water and one tablespoonful of salt into a dough and knead. Roll it out into an oval about half an inch thick. Cover it with slices of fat pork leaving the edges free. Put the fish cleaned and washed in a pile in the middle, sprinkling salt between the layers. Any kind of fish may be used for this. The country people often put quite small ones and leave them whole. The bones of these small fish become quite soft during cooking. Brush the edges of the pastry with water, lift them all together and make them meet in the middle. Press well with the fingers until the join is invisible, and the top is a smooth mound. Bake for five or six hours, and during baking baste frequently with milk. When baked, cover immediately with a towel and stand in a warm place so that the fierce heat of the centre is reduced a little. Eat with butter or sour milk. Savo is a district in the middle of Finland.

Reindeer

Reindeer meat is often larded, sprinkled with salt and pepper and put into a baking tin with sliced fried onions and water. It must be frequently basted.

Cold smoked reindeer is a favourite dish and often appears on the cold *buffet*. Smoked reindeer tongue is particularly delicious and goes well with omelets.

Index

114

WIDENER UNIVERSITY
WOLFGRAM
LIBRARY
CHESTER, PA.